A BIBLIOGRAPHY ON DIVORCE

A BIBLIOGRAPHY ON DIVORCE

Compiled and edited by
Stan Israel

Bloch Publishing Company · New York

Library of Congress Catalog Card Number: 73–77287
I.S.B.N. 0–8197–0298–6

Published by Bloch Publishing Company
915 Broadway
New York, N.Y. 10010

Manufactured in the United States of America

In Honor of
MR. AND MRS. NATHAN ISRAEL
and ROSE HERSHBERG

Contents

ACKNOWLEDGMENTS

The tireless efforts of Stephanie D. Snowden in research, typing and secretarial administration; the dependable cooperation of my brother Steven D. Israel; the guidance of attorney Steven M. Greenberg, J.D.; the consultation and advice of Frederick W. Kern, Director of the Switchboard of Miami, Inc.; the assistance of my mother, Mrs. Bessie Israel, my aunts, Miss Rose Hershberg, Mrs. Molly Leach, and Mrs. Fay Grossman, and my uncle, Mr. Alfred Leach; the typing and research endeavors of Paula Carson, Marianne Antonic, Krissi Keaton and Diane Grischy; the generous use of the facilities of the Switchboard of Miami, Inc., under its former Director, Robert J. Hintz; the consultive efforts of Marcia and Walter Jacobsen; the proofreading endeavors of Ellie Kurtz and Phyllis Byrd, Professor of English, Broward Community College; and the kind consideration of the many publishing houses granting permission to reprint data from their recent books are most gratefully acknowledged.

SAD FOR THE CHILDREN

R. Loraine Penn

Children's fair faces
Do they lie?
Children's hearts, do they say
We care? Do they say we try?
Do they know we love them?
Let us hope,
Let us pray,
Let us cry,
DIVORCE?!
Children!
Why!
We know they grow,
We both try and we both cry
For in our hearts we love them,
Our children's fair faces!!

INTRODUCTION

If divorce is of any concern to you, whether for personal or professional reasons, you will find A BIBLIOGRAPHY ON DIVORCE a practical and advantageous guide to understanding a major dilemma of modern society.

The aim of this work is to provide an easy to use general reference for those seeking either general or specialized information on divorce. Included in this comprehensive annotated bibliography are publications that deal with the many aspects of marital disharmony, separation, divorce and readjustment which have herein been categorized according to their legal, religious and sociological aspects.

Those personally involved in divorce may readily avail themselves of the vast material written on this subject and thereby be able to deal more favorably with its multiple and complex problems. Those professionally involved: lawyers, doctors, clergymen, psychologists, psychiatrists, sociologists, educators, social workers, will find this guide to publications on divorce an invaluable reference for guidance to the vast spectrum of literature on the subject.

Although every effort has been made to include all the latest material, it is understood that new and very pertinent publications on the subject are continuously becoming available. Also, some entries in the legal section may contain data that has since been updated in the courts. This new data is being collected for future publication.

Stan Israel

LEGAL ASPECTS OF DIVORCE

ALIMONY AND SUPPORT, by Stephen Bair

DELL PUBLISHING COMPANY
750 THIRD AVENUE
NEW YORK, NEW YORK 10017
1971, 25¢

Husbands and wives are tied by many strings: some legal, some emotional, some physical, some financial, but the knot that is usually most tangled is the one involving money, property and possessions. In short, nothing about separation and divorce is simple, but financial problems are often the hardest to resolve.

The aim of this book is to help women understand financial ramifications of separation and divorce. The broad principles outlined herein are generally applicable throughout the U. S. and Canada; however, readers should bear in mind that the law differs from state to state, and, even within a small town, individual judges may disagree when interpreting the law.

CONTENTS

ATTORNEY'S GUIDE TO FAMILY LAW ACT PRACTICE, by Judges Marvin A. Freeman, William P. Hogoboom, William E. MacFaden, and Lester E. Olson, with Paul M. Li

CALIFORNIA CONTINUING EDUCATION OF THE BAR
2150 SHATTUCK AVENUE
BERKELEY, CALIFORNIA 94704
1972, $30.00 300 pp.

CONTENTS

BOURKE AND FOGARTY'S MAINTENANCE, CUSTODY AND ADOPTION, by J. F. Fogarty

BUTTERWORTH & COMPANY
88 KINGSWAY
LONDON WC2B 6AB
ENGLAND
1972, $15.00 400 pp.

Maintenance, custody and adoption, being important fields of social legislation, have been the subject of continued judicial consideration and legislative amendment. The third edition aims at providing in a compact form, the relevant Commonwealth and Victorian legislation and an annotation of the more important cases bearing on the subject.

Although the book is not concerned with marriage and matrimonial causes generally, a selection has been included of relevant sections from the Commonwealth and Victorian Acts which touch upon maintenance, alimony, custody and related matters.

The scope of the third edition has been considerably widened by greater references to English and other overseas authorities making this a well rounded reference book for all those concerned with the social or legal aspects of this field.

CONTENTS

BROWN AND MORGAN'S AUSTRALIAN MATRIMONIAL CAUSES PRACTICE WITH PRECEDENTS, by A. M. Brown and K. B. Morgan

BUTTERWORTH & COMPANY
88 KINGSWAY
LONDON WC2B 6AB
ENGLAND
1971, $22.50 831 pp.

This book is a textbook for busy practical lawyers. It will quickly be recognized as a new approach to a practice book and to contain a number of features and time-saving devices not hitherto included in an Australian practice book. It is designed to get a client's case before the court with the least trouble to the solicitor, with the least cost and delay to the client, and when the case is before the court, with the utmost clarity to the court and with the greatest success to the client.

CALIFORNIA MARITAL TERMINATION SETTLEMENTS, by Stuart B. Walzer in association with Guy B. Colburn and Isadore Rosenblatt

CALIFORNIA CONTINUING EDUCATION OF THE BAR
2150 SHATTUCK AVENUE
BERKELEY, CALIFORNIA 94704
1971, $40.00 367 pp.

By agreement between the Board of Governors of the State Bar of California and the Regents of the University of California, Continuing Education of the Bar offers an educational program for the benefit of practicing lawyers. The program is administered by a Governing Committee through University of California Extension in cooperation with local bar associations and the Deans of Accredited Law Schools.

Practice books are published to accompany the various programs. Authors are given full opportunity to express their individual legal interpretations and opinions, and these obviously are not intended to reflect any position of the State Bar of California or of University Extension. Chapters written by employees of state or federal agencies are not to be considered statements of governmental policies.

CONTENTS

CALIFORNIA MARRIAGE AND DIVORCE LAWS, by Harry W. Koch

KEN BOOKS
1368 NINTH AVE.
SAN FRANCISCO, CALIFORNIA 94122
1969, $2.50 94 pp.

On September 5, 1969, Governor Reagan signed the new "Family Law Act" to become effective on January 1, 1970.

This is an entirely new concept!

Under the old law, a *divorce* was awarded to one of the parties if he or she could prove one of seven grounds. The party given the divorce, being the 'innocent' party, was usually given the larger share of the community property.

Under the new law, the parties, upon the petition of one of them, go before the court and the court may or may not decree a *dissolution of marriage.* There are only two grounds:

1. Irreconciliable differences which have caused the irremediable breakdown of the marriage.
2. Incurable insanity.

The community property is divided equally unless the court for good reason decrees otherwise.

Under the old law, *a year* of residence in the state was required in order to bring the action, and a year had to elapse between service of papers and final decree. Under the new law, it is *six months* in each case.

The principal change in the theory of the law is the elimination of the old idea of *fault.*

CONTENTS

THE NEW LAW—Summary of changes

NOTES ON THE NEW LAW by Roy A. Sharff, attorney at law

INTRODUCTION: Marriage and Divorce in general—attorneys—how California law is made—marriage and divorce in other states

THE FAMILY LAW ACT with commentaries thereon:

MARRIAGE: age of consent—licenses and solemnization—special provisions—premarital examinations, etc.

VOID AND VOIDABLE MARRIAGES:—the "judgement of nullity"

DISSOLUTION OF MARRIAGE (formerly called "Divorce"): prob-

Taken from COMPATIBLE DIVORCE, by Robert Veit Sherwin © 1969 by Robert Veit Sherwin

Used by Permission of CROWN PUBLISHERS, INC.
419 PARK AVENUE SOUTH
NEW YORK, N.Y. 10016
$5.95

Divorce need not be bitter. Here is the sensible, planned way—when divorce is inevitable—to avoid acrimony and insure the best possible arrangements for all concerned: the wife, the husband, and the children. The author is a New York divorce lawyer, who has spent his long and successful career convincing his clients that "compatible" is the word for divorce. In this book he gives invaluable guidance on choosing the right lawyer; sensible planning for the divorce; the vital need for drawing up and signing a mutually acceptable separation agreement; how to handle the problems of custody, visitation rights, and support concerning the children; necessary provisions of wills, insurance, divisions of property such as real estate and personal possessions, problems connected with remarriage of one of that couple, etc. He frankly discusses the sympathetic handling of explosive sexual problems, including homosexuality, ultraviolence, and criminal activities. And finally, he shows the compatible way of attaining the desired goal: the uncontested divorce.

What questions are uppermost in the minds of those seeking divorce? Here are ten of those asked most often. This book fully answers them and hundreds more:

1. Should the wife date during the period of separation?
2. When should the parties separate: before negotiations, just before the divorce?
3. Should the children meet the new "girlfriend" before the divorce?
4. How long should divorce negotiations take?
5. Under what circumstances can the father take custody of the child away from the mother?
6. How does the inception of the marriage affect the chances of a compatible divorce?
7. How do the sex habits of the husband and wife affect the divorce settlement?

8. How does pregnancy before marriage affect the outcome of the divorce?
9. What effect does the fact that the parties had sexual intercourse with each other prior to marriage have on the divorce negotiations?
10. How should visitation be handled during the early days of remarriage?

For all persons involved in the many aspects of divorce—clients, lawyers, judges, sociologists, marriage counselors—this book will shed new light and insight on how the act of divorce can be accomplished with minimum difficulty and maximum compatibility on the part of both husband and wife.

CONTENTS

Robert Veit Sherwin *is a practicing attorney in New York City, specializing in domestic relations, the law of literary property, real estate, estates, and psychiatry and psychology. He is the author of a number of books including "Sex and the Statutory Law," and "Legal Aspects of Photography." As a contributing author his works have appeared in many well-known volumes: "Encyclopedia of Sexual Behavior," "Sexual Behavior and the Law," "Sex Life of the American Woman," and "The Kinsey Reports," and others. He has had numerous articles published in magazines and professional journals. Among the many organizations to which he belongs are The American Academy of Matrimonial Lawyers and the American Bar Association.*

THE COMPLETE GUIDE TO DIVORCE, by Samuel G. Kling

GEIS ASSOCIATES
128 EAST 56TH ST.
NEW YORK, N.Y. 10022
1967, $6.95 305 pp. also in paper

For those who contemplate divorce, there is no substitute for this guide. It answers every possible question that might arise. The guide is written in clear layman's language, and even lawyers will find this well-organized and thorough compendium a helpful reference.

The author, Samuel Kling, is a man of many accomplishments. He has been a practicing divorce lawyer in Baltimore for more than twenty-five years. He is a distinguished and successful marriage counselor, and he is a noted writer on legal subjects.

Born in New York City, he moved with his family to the stoney stoops of Baltimore when he was nine. He began writing seriously when he was a student at the University of Baltimore Law School, and his pen has been active ever since. His feature articles have appeared in the *Baltimore Sunday Sun.* He has frequently contributed reviews to the Sunday editions of the *New York Times* and the *New York Herald Tribune,* and he has had articles published in *Look, Better Homes and Gardens,* and many other magazines. "Your Marriage", Mr. Kling's nationally syndicated column, appeared in the *New York World-Telegram,* the *Chicago Daily News,* and fifty-five other leading newspapers for eight years.

Mr. Kling is also the author of "The Complete Guide to Everyday Law" and "Your Will and What To Do About It". Both are published by Follet Publishing Company.

CONTENTS

CONCEPT OF MATRIMONIAL CRUELTY, by John M. Briggs

THE ATHLONE PRESS, UNIVERSITY OF LONDON
4 GOWER STREET
LONDON WC1E 6DR, ENGLAND
1962

The law of cruelty has received considerable attention from the courts, especially in recent years, and decisions follow each other (chronologically speaking) with almost bewildering rapidity. The basic object in writing this book has been to draw together the general principles underlying the concept of cruelty and to remove the emphasis from the many individual cases reported in which the only novelty appears to lie in the facts found rather than in the law applied. Consequently, although all the significant cases on cruelty have been included, the coverage is not exhaustive; I trust that it has thereby avoid being exhausting to a reader whilst remaining a useful work of reference to those who practice in this branch of law.

CONTENTS

DIVORCE, by Raoul Lionel Felder Copyright © 1971 by Raoul Lionel Felder

THE WORLD PUBLISHING COMPANY
110 EAST 59TH STREET
NEW YORK, NEW YORK 10019
1971, $7.20 263 pp.

Marriages may be made in heaven, but divorces are not. "Anyone who lives through the excruciating internal debate as to whether or not to divorce, and what to expect if he does, is entitled to be told what the situation actually is," says Attorney Raoul Lionel Felder. In "Divorce," he describes the anatomy of divorce from its troubled beginnings to its sometimes equally troubled aftermath. The causes and problems are as varied as the people they affect, and the author draws his examples from the very real men and women whose cases he has handled.

He begins his analysis of divorce before it reaches the lawyer's office when the hidden resentments may have begun to surface in the sexual area of the marriage. He considers the possibilities of counseling and, if divorce has become inevitable, what a lawyer can do, what he needs to know about the case, and what happens when a case goes to court. He interviews a detective who tells his own experiences in gathering evidence of adultery, the mechanics of raiding a love nest, and how much such investigations cost. Mr. Felder explains how he attacks a case, presents it before judge or jury to capitalize on the law, the marriage relationship and the stakes of the litigants, and how the parties react when it is over.

But this is not a "how to" book; it is a "how it is" book. Attorney Felder is concerned with the human beings he has seen in their most vulnerable moments, torn by the ego-smashing realities of divorce: the women swinging from vindictiveness to dependence; the men indulging themselves while deviously hiding their true income from their wives; the "nouveau—riche" who part so painfully with their money; the long wealthy who settle so easily; the neurotics, the psychotics; the willing victims and the shrewd exploiters. He must deal with them all, and he tells frankly how he does. He works within the system, and, as a lawyer, his goal is always to get the best terms for his client—whether or not society is best served by the results. This is why he concludes this book with a chapter on "how it should be"—his own startling ideas about how society can change the divorce laws so that both parties, their children, and society emerge from the contest with fewer tragic consequences.

CONTENTS

APPENDIX

Felder *is a practicing attorney in New York and is a Fellow of the American Academy of Matrimonial Lawyers. He originally studied medicine and later took up law. As a Federal Prosecutor during the Kennedy years, he prosecuted major criminal cases on behalf of the Government. He travels extensively and during the early 1950's lived in Switzerland. An incessant reader, Mr. Felder is also a gourmet and has a collection of over 700 cookbooks!*

DIVORCE AND AFTER, by Gerald P. Sanctuary and Constance Christina Whitehead

VICTOR GOLLANCZ, LTD.
14 HENRIETTA STREET
CONVENT GARDEN
LONDON WC2, ENGLAND
1970, £1.40

Divorce: it's the word we use to mean the legal ending of a marriage, but in fact it means a lot more than that. It represents the end of the hopes that two people had for each other; it's the certificate that their relationship failed. It is not just a matter of law; it is about people under stress. And many of these divorced and separated people find themselves in an unpleasant situation with little idea of how to cope with it. So many problems are liable to arise, emotional and practical. So many people need help and don't quite know where to turn for it. This book, a handbook for divorced people, provides that help, in all the areas where help is possible. Its authors are very well qualified to write it: Gerald Sanctuary has been a lawyer, is the author of "Marriage Under Stress", and was until recently General Secretary of the National Marriage Guidance Council; Constance Whitehead is an experienced journalist and has been much involved in administration of clubs for divorced people. As they frankly write, "Nothing we can say will make the situation pleasant [But] we can help you to see the situation for what it is; we can show how it is possible to recreate a life of meaning from what seemed to be a total disaster; and we can give in detail the various ways in which support can be found."

CONTENTS

DIVORCE AND ANNULMENT IN THE 50 STATES, by Michael F. Mayer

ARCO PUBLISHING CO., INC.
219 PARK AVENUE SOUTH
NEW YORK, N.Y. 10003
Revised Edition 1971, $1.45 paperback

This concise examination of all legal aspects of ending a marriage covers:

CAUSES FOR DIVORCE OR ANNULMENT:

Absence, adultery, bigamy, crime, cruelty, desertion, discretion of the court, diseases, drunkenness or narcotics, duress, foreign divorce, fraud in marriage, impotence, incompatability, indignities, insanity or mental incapacity, intoxication, living apart, miscegenation, non-support, pregnancy by another, under-age marriage.

DEFENSES TO COMPLAINTS:

Clean hands, co-habitation, collusion, condonation, connivance, estoppel, insanity, limitations of time, living under same roof pending trial, not married, pre-marital knowledge, provocation, recrimination, separation agreements.

CONSENT

OUT OF STATE AND FOREIGN DIVORCES

ALIMONY

CUSTODY

CHILD SUPPORT

Michael F. Mayer *is partner in the New York law firm of Spring & Mayer and former Executive Director of Independent Film Importers of America. He has also written "Foreign Films on American Screens" and "What You Should Know About Libel & Slander," both published by ARCO.*

DIVORCE AND CUSTODY FOR MEN, by Charles V. Metz (Guide & primer designed exclusively for men to help win just settlements)

DOUBLEDAY, 1968
out of print at this time

This is an unchivalrous book. It has one purpose: to help defend the rights of husbands against the injustices that are endemic in our divorce system. In other words, it is a book designed to protect husbands from their divorced wives to-be. And it pulls no punches. It tells you how to recognize the danger signals in your marriage—the signs that the "little woman" has her eye on greener pastures. It tells you when and how to beat her to the punch and file for divorce yourself. It is a practical guide to the selection of a lawyer, to the conduct of your divorce proceedings, to gaining custody of the children, to an equitable alimony arrangement, to gaining reasonably prompt court action—and, hopefully, to a verdict in your favor and against your wife.

"Divorce and Custody" is, above all, a book unabashedly and exclusively for men. It provides the means to fight hard and intelligently against the scandalous inequalities of the divorce system in America with respect to a husband's—or ex-husband's—rights. "Do these things," says the author, "and you may not be burned. If you are right, fight to win." With the inside knowledge this book provides, you have a good chance of doing so.

CONTENTS

1. Friends, Romans and Countrymen
2. Till Death Do Us Apart
3. The Facts of Life
4. Pre-Storm Signals
5. Divorce Costs Money
6. Who Files First?
7. You Have Your Rights, Responsibilities, Liabilities, and Alternatives
8. It Takes Guts to Choose a Good Lawyer
9. The Care and Nourishment of Attorneys
10. Alimony, the Shameful Vice
11. The Courts and Social Workers
12. All's Fair in Love, War, and Custody

Charles V. Metz *has spent a good deal of his life helping men through divorce proceedings. He is active in an organization which specializes in advising men with divorce problems and is an avid campaigner for judicial and legislative reform of divorce laws.*

DIVORCE AND YOU, by Walter T. Winter, LL.B.

THE MACMILLAN COMPANY
866 THIRD AVE.
NEW YORK, N.Y. 10022
1963, $2.95

"Divorce granted." With these words, one out of every four marriages comes to an end. Often, the tragedy of a broken home is needlessly increased by the participants' lack of knowledge about the laws, the realities, and the aftermath of divorce. This book describes simply and authoritatively the basic problems and procedures involved in having your marriage dissolved by the courts. Written by an eminent divorce attorney, it explains, step-by-step, each phase of the divorce process, from the time it is instituted to the time the judge signs the decree.

How do you pick a lawyer? How much will he charge? What are the grounds for divorce in your state? What about custody of the children? In answering these and many other questions, Walter T. Winter describes every type of court action from amicable settlement to bitterly contested battle. He discusses the legal foundations for the dissolution of a marriage, annulments, and "quickie" divorces which were legal at one time in Nevada, Alabama, and Mexico. He tells you how best to serve your case by co-operating with your lawyer, how to be a good witness, and how to avoid mistakes while testifying.

What about alimony and child support? With sympathetic understanding for each of the parties concerned, Mr. Winter discusses the methods of enforcing payment and the problems involved in minimizing adverse effects on children during litigation. He explains the Division of Property Laws in both Community Property and Common Law states and lists the special provisions for property settlements, alimony, and child support set up by the Bureau of Internal Revenue.

The final chapter offers constructive and encouraging advice on your new status in the community, relationships with your children and ex-spouse, how to handle loneliness, and your chances for a successful second marriage. A useful summary of marriage laws and the major grounds for divorce, separation and annulment in each of the fifty states, as well as a glossary of legal terms, is included at the end of the book.

"Divorce and You" is essential reading for anyone either considering a divorce or in the process of getting one. It is not a substitute for a competent attorney. It does, however, provide the important background you need to prepare yourself for the difficult task of facing and understanding the realities of your divorce.

CONTENTS

THE DIVORCE HANDBOOK, by Florence Haussamen and Mary Ann Guitar

G.P. PUTNAM'S SONS 1960
out of print at this time

Each year, it has been estimated, 350,000 Americans take the crucial step of divorce. But, no one can estimate the countless thousands who contemplate divorce, who seek information, who need counsel on their marriage and their future. It is for these thousands of men and women that this book has been written.

As Judge Alexander says in his Foreword, "The purpose of this book is not to make divorce easier but to make it more easily understood." Here is the key information, legal and practical, on all subjects: from legal grounds for divorce to what to do about children, from the separation agreement to alimony and other financial matters, from marriage counseling to legal advice. Here, too, are easy-to-use charts giving important data to readers from any one of the fifty states. Never before has so much essential material on divorce been made available in a single, readable, accurate, unmoralizing book. "The Divorce Handbook" is truly the first layman's service book on divorce.

CONTENTS

Florence Haussamen *has been a radio and television script writer for a number of years and has done educational publicity for Northwestern University, Columbia Teachers College and the Conference on Science, Philosophy and Religion. Her writings have appeared in* Harper's Bazaar, Reader's Digest, New York Times, Coronet, *and numerous other publications.*

Mary Ann Guitar, *at one time Senior Editor for Articles at* Woman's Home Companion *and previously* Woman's Day *and* House and Garden, *now devotes full time to free-lance writing. Her name will be familiar to readers of virtually all the popular women's magazines now being published in America.*

DIVORCE IN THE "LIBERAL" JURISDICTIONS, by David Von G. Albrecht

FEDERAL LEGAL PUBLICATIONS, INC.
NEW YORK, N.Y.
1955, $2.50

One of the thoughts with which people in the northeastern part of the United States have deluded themselves is that the inhabitants of their area are actually bound by rigid rules concerning divorce. But in the other areas of the country, such as Alabama, Florida, Nevada, and the Virgin Islands, the rigid rules don't seem to apply, and of greater interest is the fact that the less restrictive approach is increasingly available to all.

CONTENTS

David Von G. Albrecht *is the chairman of our special Committee on Marriage and Divorce, and he has arranged for an expert on matters of divorce from each of the aforementioned areas to present to you the facts. The Federal Bar Association of New York, New Jersey and Connecticut will welcome comment thereon.*

THE DIVORCE LAWYERS' CASEBOOK, by Robert and Lawrence Kahn

ST. MARTIN'S PRESS
175 FIFTH AVENUE
NEW YORK, NEW YORK 10010
1972, $5.95

"Divorce is a cop-out, only freeing the individuals to take the same problems to a new setting." So say Robert and Lawrence Kahn, who have handled thousands of divorce proceedings in their combined thirty years of practice.

The authors have seen the same patterns emerge time and time again, although each couple going through a marital breakup undoubtedly considers their predicament unprecedented. They wrote the book at the repeated urgings of clients, some of whose marriages they were able to save and others who endured bitter, contested divorce actions. "The Divorce Lawyers' Casebook" was written to give those contemplating a divorce action some idea of what they face.

Each of the case histories included here is factual and based on a combination of several similar cases the authors have handled. Names and locales have been changed to protect the privacy of those involved. The cases range from mental cruelty actions to bizarre cases of sexual behavior (one woman got a divorce after she testified that her husband had been intimate with a chicken.)

Within the context of the cases the authors consider marital danger signals, how to go about reconciling "irreconcilable" differences, and common myths about marriage and divorce. They also discuss counselling, picking a lawyer, family court, legal separation, divorce proceedings, divorce and children and remarriage.

CONTENTS

Robert W. Kahn *was born in Troy, New York, in 1927 and received a B.A degree from Siena College in 1948 and an L.L.B. degree from Albany Law School in 1951. He began practicing law that year.*

Lawrence E. Kahn *was born in Troy, New York in 1937. He received a B.A. degree from Union College in 1959 and L.L.B. and J.D. degrees from Harvard Law School in 1962. He did post-graduate legal work for one year at Oxford University, England. In 1963 he returned to Albany, New York, to join his brother in the practice of law. He is a member of the New York State Bar Asociation's Family Law Committee.*

Their law firm, Kahn and Kahn, has handled thousands of divorce cases since its formation in 1963 and they have handled thousands of divorce cases. Both brothers are members of the Albany County, New York State and American Bar Associations and are Fellows of the American Academy of Matrimonial Lawyers.

Lawrence E. Kahn is active in civic and political affairs and was honored in 1967 as one of New York State's "five outstanding young men." He and his wife, the former Michele Kagan, a speech therapist, have two daughters, Tamara and Alyssa. Robert W. Kahn and his wife, the former Ilene N. Weiss, have a son Jeffrey and a daughter Marcy.

DIVORCE PROBLEMS HANDBOOK, by Frederick M. Kal and Harry A. Frumess

FREDERICK FELL, INC., 1961
out of print at this time

More than 800,000 matrimonial cases come before our courts each year, and approximately half of these actions result in divorce. This number is on the increase, so that today divorce is the most crucial maladjustment threatening the American Family.

This deteriorating situation is receiving ever greater attention from educational groups and religious institutions, the medical profession, and social agencies.

Yet the couple considering divorce—and sometimes the agencies advising them—are often woefully ignorant of the specific details of the laws governing the grave act they contemplate. Small wonder—when the divorce laws of our 50 states vary so widely, and to the layman often seem unbelievably complex. What both the layman considering divorce and the professional counselor need is some clarification of the basic issues surrounding the problem.

This book is an attempt to meet that urgent need—a clear, concrete survey, in layman's language, of the problems relating to divorce—to make the troubled marriage partner aware of what is to be faced—and to provide legally sound information for the minister and physician, the psychologist and psychiatrist, the marriage counselor and social worker.

Here then, are the 1200 questions and answers that most commonly arise in connection with an action for divorce, annulment or separation, prepared by two eminent members of the American Bar.

They cover every major aspect of the problem, and its minor interpretations contingent upon special circumstances and local law.

——Grounds for divorce; ranging from the common—adultery, cruelty and desertion—to the most unusual—wife's pregnancy from another man, "crimes against nature," being a member of a religious sect forbidding cohabitation. . . .

——Defenses to defeat a divorce action from insanity to collusion; from provocation to acts of cruelty, to condonation or forgiveness of adulterous or other offensive acts. . . .

——Alimony and Support money: The difference between temporary support money and permanent alimony; the question of attorneys' fees; the enforcement of alimony decrease when delinquency occurs.

——Child custody and support: One of the most bitterly disputed areas in divorce proceedings, and the laws which govern it. . . .

——Out-of-State and Out-of-Country divorces: Their legal validity in a population which has become both more mobile and more prone to seek "foreign" divorces. . . .

——Financial and economic agreements: Problems relating to property division, taxes, inheritance and bankruptcy. . . .

——Divorce, annulment or separate maintenance? How they basically differ, the special grounds required for each, and the commitments each entails. . . .

In addition, concise summaries are given of the divorce laws in each of the 50 states, as well as a glossary of legal terms in common use in divorce actions.

This book is in no sense intended as a substitute for an attorney's services. Divorce is not a "do-it-yourself" project. Nor is it, on the other hand, a project into which every unhappily married person should lead blindly, in search of a quick and easy solution to his problems, without giving long and serious thought to the consequences.

And, because so many threatened marriages can *be salvaged by forethought and foreknowledge, this comprehensive guide closes with a section devoted to the kind of assistance that is available to those whose marriages are in trouble, and where they are most likely to find valuable aid.*

Frederick M. Kal *attended the University of Denver and Colorado State College. He is a graduate of Westminister College of Law and has been in the practice of law since 1946. He is a member of the Denver Bar Association, Colorado Bar Association, American Bar Association, and the American Bar Association Section on Family Law.*

Harry A. Frumess *is a graduate of the University of Colorado and the University of Denver Law School and has been in the practice of law since 1940. He is a member of the Denver, Colorado and American Bar Association and the American Judicature Society and has contributed articles to legal publications.*

THE DIVORCE RACKET, by Stanley Rosenblatt

Copyright © by NASH PUBLISHING
9255 SUNSET BOULEVARD
LOS ANGELES, CALIF. 90069
1969, $5.95 Reprinted by permission of Nash Publishing, Los Angeles, Calif.

Divorce is one of the most serious problems facing our society today. Archaic laws governing divorce in the 50 states are confusing and unfair, especially to the husband.

Each state has its own particular set of laws. What may constitute legal grounds for divorce in one state may not in another. Archaic laws in most states have forced thousands to perjure themselves or to seek a divorce in a state or country with more liberal laws.

America's outmoded divorce laws are hopelessly out of step with our modern society. The author brings to light the gravity of the divorce problem in our country. Grounds and defenses in the various states are discussed. An entire chapter is devoted to the subject of alimony. Included are two historic divorce cases that vividly point out the cruel injustices which are inflicted upon people merely because they have selected the wrong mate.

There are millions of Americans who know that divorce laws in this country are a national disgrace. This book analyzes the faults and absurdities of our existing system and proposes a revolutionary and practical alternative.

CONTENTS

Stanley Rosenblatt *is a partner in the law firm Granat, Rosenblatt, & Roemer, Miami, Florida. Since he began private practice, he has specialized as a trial attorney in the negligence or personal injury field. His dislike of divorce litigation inspired him to write this timely book.*

DIVORCE REFORM LAW, by Professor Henry H. Foster, Jr., and Dr. Jonas Freed

LAWYER'S CO-OPERATIVE PUBLISHING COMPANY
AQUEDUCT BUILDING
ROCHESTER, NEW YORK 14603
1970, 66 pp.

The first major revision since 1787 of the substantive law of divorce in New York (Ch. 254, L. of 1966) was enacted by the legislature and signed by the Governor on April 27, 1966. Most of the new law became effective on September 1, 1967, including the new grounds for divorce. However, under section 15 of the new Act the specified time of two years of living apart under new section 170 (5) and (6) of the Domestic Relations Law commenced to operate as of September 1, 1966, with the first possiblity of divorce on such grounds being September 1, 1968, due to the stipulation of section 15 that the two year period "shall not be computed to include any period prior to September 1, 1966." Moreover, sections 10 and 12 of the new law became effective as of April 27, 1966, the former being the new section 235 of the Domestic Relations Law relating to the confidentiality of the details of matrimonial proceedings, and the latter the amendment to section 5–311 of the General Obligation Law which clarifies or mitigates the effect of VILES V VILES, 14 NY2d 365,200 NE2d 567, 251 NYS2d 672 (1964), and proscribes only express agreements to obtain a divorce.

The new law grew out of the 219 page report of the Joint Legislative Committee on Matrimonial and Family Laws, commonly called the "Wilson Committee," which was dated March 31, 1966. The Joint Committee was established pursuant to a joint resolution dated June 8, 1965. In addition to its report, the Committee sponsored legislation which was introduced at the 1966 legislative session in both the Senate and the House, which was commonly referred to as the Wilson-Sutton Bill. Alternative legislation was introduced by Senators Travia, Huges, and Brydges which defered substantially from the earlier proposal. The latter bill was commonly referred to as the "Leader's Bill." Thereafter, compromises were effected between the sponsors of the competing bills and the law which was finally enacted contained features taken from both bills.

A comment will be made on each of the important sections of

the new law and an effort will be made to discern probable legislative intent. In the absence of the transcript of the Senate and Assembly debates on April 27, 1966, and lacking any printed report from the Committee on Rules or the Judiciary Committee, references to probable legislative meaning or intent necessarily are speculative and there is no official authority for any attributions of legislative meaning.

CONTENTS

ESCAPE FROM MARRIAGE, by Donald J. Cantor

WILLIAM MORROW & CO.
105 MADISON AVENUE
NEW YORK, N.Y. 10016
1971, $4.95 191 pp.

In this country one out of every four marriages ends in divorce. Each year more than 800,000 Americans discover our divorce laws are obsolete, illogical, and unnecessarily cruel. We live in a time of sweeping social change. There is widespread demand for divorce reform, and progress is painfully slow.

This outspoken book examines the process of divorce thoughtfully. It explains the legal implications of the marriage contract and the special divorce laws in different states. It focuses on the evils of the adversary system requiring charge and proof of fault. It shows how the resulting bargaining often prevents justice and makes children the innocent victims of divorce. Case histories are included to illustrate vividly the strategies of lawyers and to explain what one spouse can do to another with the weapons of the divorce law as it now stands.

Everyone who has known intimately the everyday cruelty of divorce should read this book and consider its recommendations for reform. It will be of inestimable help to anyone who is considering divorce (or marriage). Ministers, marriage counselors, sociologists, lawyers, and lawmakers will find it of especial interest.

CONTENTS

Donald J. Cantor, *a graduate of Harvard College and Harvard Law School, has had a private law practice since 1959 in Hartford, Connecticut. He served in the U.S. Navy from 1956 to 1959.*

An experienced divorce lawyer, Mr. Cantor has lectured and written extensively in the area of divorce, abortion, homosexuality, and censorship law. He is the author of an essay entitled "The Right of Divorce" that was published in The Atlantic *in November 1966. Another essay by Mr. Cantor on divorce reform was published in the May-June 1970 issue of* The Humanist.

THE FAMILY AND THE LAW, by Sarah T. Knox

THE UNIVERSITY OF NORTH CAROLINA PRESS
CHAPEL HILL, NORTH CAROLINA 27514
1941, $2.00 199 pp.

The following pages have been written with the hope that they will bring to social workers and interested laymen a better understanding of the fundamentals of our legal system, and of the reasons back of its development.

In a general sense there is no division of the law that does not relate to human beings or some aspect of living. Negotiable instruments, corporation law, and insurance—to mention only a few examples—in some way and at some time affect the lives of all of us. Since there had to be a selection and limitation, only those sections of law which affect the family most directly have been considered, for it is in these fields that legal information is of the greatest value to social workers. Though the chapters on criminal law, procedure, and evidence may not seem to affect the family very closely, they were included in order to give some idea of the working mechanics of the law.

CONTENTS

Sarah T. Knox *has had the background of personal experience as an administrator of a social agency and training in the study of law which makes this useful book possible. She writes with clearness, tolerance, and freedom from personal prejudices; therefore, her book reveals that practicality which has had so much to do with her successful career in social administration.*

FAMILY LAW, by C. Clinton Clad, Harry M. Halstead, and Donald W. Crocker

AMERICAN LEGAL INSTITUTE/AMERICAN BAR ASSOCIATION
4025 CHESTNUT STREET
PHILADELPHIA, PENNSYLVANIA 19104
1964

"Family Law" is a comprehensive practice handbook for counseling in the area of personal and financial problems arising from the family relationship.

CONTENTS

The authors of this, the third edition, have greatly expanded the tax treatment of individual members of the family, of intrafamily transactions, and of changes in the family status, and have devoted a separate chapter to the taxation of the head of the household.

FAMILY LAW IN ASIA AND AFRICA, Edited by J.N.D. Anderson

FREDERICK PRAEGER, PUBLISHERS
111 FOURTH AVENUE
NEW YORK, N.Y. 10003
1968, $12.50

We are witnessing today a new—and welcome—emphasis on comparative law, together with a quickened interest in the law of family relations, both in the universities and the practicing profession. This book provides a wealth of information for those who wish to study the laws of family relations within a widely comparative context.

This book covers the basic laws of marriage and divorce in a number of developing African and Asian nations, and it also discusses in considerable detail the ways in which family property is regulated under different systems. In addition, it treats many related topics: the eclipse of the patriarchal family in contemporary Islamic law; religious law and the family in modern Israel; the juristic basis and context of Parsi family law; and contemporary family law in Southern Africa.

The contributors, outstanding authorities in their fields, include Haji Ahmad Ibrahim, former Attorney General of Singapore; H.R. Hahlo, an eminent authority on Roman-Dutch law; Professor Z. W. Falk, of the Hebrew University in Jerusalem; Ludo Rocher, an eminent Indologist; Professor Maurice Freedman, of the London School of Economics; and Professor Phiroze Irani, formerly of the University of Bombay—together with most of the teaching staff of the Department of Law at the School of Oriental and African Studies, London.

CONTENTS

5. The Theory of Matrimonial Causes According to the Dharmasastra —Ludo Rocher

PART TWO FAMILY PROPERTY AND SUCCESSION

6. Family Property in West Africa: Its Juristic Basis, Control and Enjoyment—A.N. Allott
7. The Matrimonial Regimes of South Africa—H.R. Hahlo
8. Family Arrangements in Developing Countries—J.D.M. Derrett
9. The Muslims in Malaysia and Singapore: The Law of Matrimonial Property—Anche Ahmad Ibrahim
10. Community of Property in the Marriage Law of Burma—Alan Gledhill

PART THREE GENERAL

11. The Eclipse of the Patriarchal Family in Contemporary Islamic Law—J.N.D. Anderson
12. Religious Law and the Modern Family in Israel—Z.W. Falk
13. Customary Family Law in Southern Africa: Its Place and Scope—Neville Rubin
14. The Personal Law of the Parsis of India—Phiroze K. Irani

J.N.D. Anderson *is Professor of Oriental Laws, Director of the Institute of Advanced Legal Studies, and Dean of the Faculty of Laws at the University of London.*

FINLAY & BISSETT-JOHNSON'S FAMILY LAW IN AUSTRALIA, by H. A. Finlay and A. Bissett-Johnson

BUTTERWORTH & COMPANY
88 KINGSWAY
LONDON WC2B 6AB, ENGLAND
$16.00 hard; $12.50 soft 600 pp. n. d.

Extensively researched and fully annotated, the authors examine in a highly readable style all aspects of Family Law. Covering a much wider field than the average textbook, it represents an important new departure in the treatment of this topic in that Family Law is dealt with for the first time in the setting of the relevant social/historical background with emphasis on the sociological aspects. The practising lawyer will find the wide scope and clear and accurate treatment of existing law of the greatest assistance while social workers and marriage counsellors will receive guidance from the strong sociological content. There is informed criticism of aspects of the existing matrimonial law and an entire chapter is devoted to a thought-provoking discussion on the future developments of Family Law with emphasis on desirable reforms. A number of up-to-date statistical tables have been included.

CONTENTS

GETTING A VIRGINIA DIVORCE, by William B. Clinch

DENLINGER'S
P.O. BOX 76, FAIRFAX, VA. 22030
1970, $2.50

If you are contemplating or are faced with a divorce in Virginia or you are a Virginia resident contemplating a divorce elsewhere, this text will enlighten you as to your rights and your obligations in the divorce action. Clients do not get enough legal advice; lawyers simply do not have the time to give full explanations of their reasoning at each stage of the action and to do the legal work, too. In addition, many divorce clients resist hearing what their lawyer has to say; an unhappy, anxious client is too upset to absorb much of what the lawyer says.

If you have retained an attorney, this volume will help you to understand and to remember what he has said. If you have not consulted an attorney, it will acquaint you with the general rules governing Virginia divorces. In either event, this volume is not a substitute for your lawyer's legal advice; it is intended to supplement that advice, to assist you in understanding it, and therefore, to reduce your anxiety during a difficult period.

CONTENTS

William Clinch, *41, received his B.A. degree from Yale and his law degree from George Washington University, Washington, D.C.. Coming from Charlottesville, he has lived in and practiced law in Northern Virginia since 1957. He concentrates on litigation and belongs to both the Virginia and the District of Columbia bars.*

HOW TO DO YOUR OWN DIVORCE IN CALIFORNIA, WITH FORMS, by Charles E. Sherman

NOLO PRESS
BOX X 2147, STATION A
BERKELEY, CALIFORNIA 94702
$5.25 (includes postage) 89 pp. n. d.

This book will help you decide whether or not you need an attorney. If you do not, it will show you how to do your own divorce.

Do not try to do your own divorce if your spouse will oppose it, nor where you have unresolved problems with child custody, child support, spousal support (alimony) or division of the marital property, nor when your spouse is in active military service, nor if your spouse cannot be located.

A set of forms and instructions can be obtained from the publisher.

CONTENTS

C. CHILDREN: CUSTODY AND VISITATION

C1–Generally

C2–Custody

C3–Visitation

D. CHILD SUPPORT AND SPOUSAL SUPPORT (ALIMONY)

PART TWO: HOW TO DO YOUR OWN DISSOLUTION

1. HOW TO USE THE FORMS
2. CHECK LIST—HOW TO DO YOUR OWN DISSOLUTION
3. HOW TO FILE PAPERS
4. THE STATISTICAL FORM
5. THE SUMMONS
6. THE PETITION
7. THE CONFIDENTIAL QUESTIONNAIRE
8. HOW TO SERVE PAPERS ON YOUR SPOUSE
9. THE PROOF OF SERVICE
10. THE REQUEST FOR DEFAULT
11. THE HEARING
12. THE INTERLOCUTORY JUDGMENT
13. THE NOTICE OF ENTRY OF JUDGMENT
14. THE REQUEST FOR FINAL JUDGMENT
15. THE FINAL JUDGMENT

11 BLANK FORMS—for doing your own dissolution

Attorney Charles E. Sherman *thinks the uncontested divorce should cost less than $50.*

He's making that possible for Californians with his new handbook, "How to Do Your Divorce."

The tall, lanky 33-year-old also has other ideas that may stir up the dust on old law traditions.

"The legal system is so rarely responsive to the needs of the average man," said Sherman, adding, "I hope that doesn't make me a radical."

His philosophy is that "the practice of law is a life function and not a license to make money."

Shy-mannered, gentle-voiced, with ear-length sandy hair and a shaggy mustache, Sherman wore boots, jeans, a casual shirt as he talked in the modest Berkeley cottage that is office and home. His neighbors' numerous children, pets and chickens provided homespun background noises.

ILLINOIS DIVORCE, SEPARATE MAINTENANCE AND ANNULMENT, by Meyer Weinberg

THE BOBBS-MERRILL COMPANY, INC.
4300 WEST 62ND ST.
INDIANAPOLIS, IND. 46268
1969, $25.00

CONTENTS

Meyer Weinberg, *LLB, DePaul University College of Law, has been a member of the Illinois Bar since 1934, and since 1958, Editor of the Family Law Bulletin of the Illinois State Bar Association. He has been a frequent contributor to legal periodicals on the subject of family law, and has frequently lectured on family law before bar association groups in Illinois. With over thirty years trial experience in family law, he is known as a "lawyer's lawyer."*

JACKSON'S FORMATION AND ANNULMENT OF MARRIAGE, by Joseph Jackson

BUTTERWORTH & COMPANY
88 KINGSWAY
LONDON WC2B 6AB
ENGLAND
1969, $21.18

This book deals in detail with all legal problems relating to marriage and nullity, and explains both the historical background and the modern law. Bigamy, affinity and consanguinity, age of marriage, parental consent to marriage, and consent of the parties themselves are among the topics examined, as well as the formalities of marriage and non-consummation. The bars to relief are examined fully, and jurisdiction and recognition are described in the appropriate chapters.

CONTENTS

The author, who is Editor-in-Chief of Rayden (see p. 52), is an authority on this branch of the law and writes with insight and clarity. For all who require a fundamental background to matrimonial law, as well as an up-to-date description of marriage law in England, this book is essential.

JACKSON'S MATRIMONIAL FINANCE AND TAXATION, by Joseph Jackson, M.A.

BUTTERWORTH & COMPANY
88 KINGSWAY
LONDON WC2B 6AB
ENGLAND
1972, $26.95

This book is about the financial and taxation aspects of marriage breakdowns and consequential procedures necessary to evaluate in cash terms the basis upon which a divorce decree or court order should be granted. There must be very few lawyers or accountants in public practice who do not at some time or another find themselves involved in computing what payments to a spouse ought to be recommended to the Court. The author states that in many cases there is insufficient recourse to the accountant: also there is insufficient knowledge of the principles to be applied.

The book deals with the procedures which have to be followed in litigation and the taxation aspects of a Court order.

The author, well-known for his editorship of "Rayden on Divorce," has long thought that too little attention has been given to matrimonial financial matters. All too often the processes by which financial orders and agreements are reached are hit-and-miss and haphazard. Considering the enormous number of persons involved in matrimonial financial disputes, this is an alarming state of affairs.

JOSKE'S MATRIMONIAL CAUSES AND MARRIAGE LAW AND PRACTICE OF AUSTRALIA AND NEW ZEALAND, by P. E. Joske

BUTTERWORTH & COMPANY
88 KINGSWAY
LONDON WC2B 6AB
ENGLAND

FIFTH EDITION 1969 with
1970 SUPPLEMENT

$25.00 (including Supplement)—951 pp.
$5.00 (Supplement only)

An interpretation of the law by case history and legal precedent, the first section consists of a comprehensive treatise arranged to facilitate easy reference with extensive footnotes. The second section sets out the Matrimonial Causes Act 1959–1966 with expert annotations and all the schedules relating to that Act.

The Third Edition has been updated by the 1970 Supplement which covers over three hundred cases, with citations indicating exactly where the full report is to be found. Joske's monumental work is the leading textbook in the field of marriage and divorce.

KNOW YOUR RIGHTS UNDER NEW YORK'S NEW DIVORCE LAW, by Parnell Joseph Terrence Callahan

OCEANA PUBLICATIONS, INC.
DOBBS FERRY, N.Y. 10522
1966, $1.50

WHEN DID THE LAW GO INTO EFFECT?
ON WHAT GROUNDS WILL DIVORCE BE GRANTED?
WHAT IS CRUELTY?
HOW LONG MUST ABANDONMENT CONTINUE TO AUTHORIZE A DIVORCE?
MAY A DIVORCE BE GRANTED FOR CONFINEMENT IN PRISON?
WHAT IS ADULTERY?
MAY A DIVORCE BE GRANTED AFTER A LEGAL SEPARATION?
CAN MY WIFE AND I AGREE TO GET A DIVORCE?
ARE DIVORCE CASES TRIED BEFORE JURIES?
HOW IS A DIVORCE CASE STARTED?
WHY MUST THERE BE A SPECIAL GUARDIAN FOR CHILDREN?
IS A CONCILIATION CONFERENCE REQUIRED?
HOW LONG DOES IT TAKE TO GET A DIVORCE?
MAY I REMARRY AFTER DIVORCE?
ARE OUT OF STATE VOICES VALID?
WHAT HAPPENS IN A MEXICAN DIVORCE?

CONTENTS

Parnell J. T. Callahan, *A.B., L.L.B., Columbia University; former faculty member of Queens College, United States Army Judge Advocate General School, and Seton Hall University Law School; member of the United States Army Judiciary, Judge Advocate General Corps., United States Army Reserve; practicing lawyer in New York State since 1937. Admitted to practice in United States Supreme Court and United States Court of Military Appeals.*

LAW AND PRACTICE IN MATRIMONIAL CAUSES, by Bernard Passingham

BUTTERWORTH & COMPANY
88 KINGSWAY
LONDON WC2B 6AB
ENGLAND
1971, $21.18 casebound; $13.86 limp

A plethora of diverse and complex legislation relating to matrimonial causes has recently come into effect. This new book provides a guide to the developments in this branch of the law, compensating for the scarcity of reported cases which would show how the law was working in practice. The author originally intended to write this book as a textbook for students. However, in the course of discussions with practising solicitors and legal executives while writing the book, he realized that they, too, needed the information which it contains. He has therefore considered the needs of both practitioners and students, covering both the law and practice in matrimonial causes.

CONTENTS

LAW FOR THE FAMILY MAN, by Libby F. Jessup

OCEANA PUBLICATIONS, U.S.A.
DOBBS FERRY, N.Y. 10522
1958,

This is the forty-fifth volume in the Legal Almanac series. These almanacs bring the law on various subjects to you in non-technical language. They do not take the place of your attorney, but they can introduce you to your legal rights and responsibilities.

CONTENTS

LAW IN FAMILY CONFLICT, by Samuel Abrahams

LAW-ARTS PUBLISHERS, INC.
453 GREENWICH STREET
NEW YORK, NEW YORK 10038
1970, 287 pp.

This book attempts to give the reader a glimpse into some unique, bizarre and vital sectors of marital, family and social welfare law. The author states that he does not follow the pattern one is apt to find in a conventional textbook or legal treatise on this subject that describes in detail every conceivable angle and procedural device a litigant is bound to encounter in the judicial tug of war known as matrimonial conflict.

CONTENTS

Samuel Abrahams *is a 46 year-old native of New York. He is a practicing lawyer with specialties in Family Constitutional Law and related areas. He is an honors graduate of Brooklyn College (BA), Columbia University (MA), Brooklyn Law School (JD), and the New York University School of Law (LLM).*

THE LAW OF SEPARATION AND DIVORCE, by Parnell Joseph Terrence Callahan

OCEANA PUBLICATIONS, INC.
DOBBS FERRY, N.Y. 10522
1970, $3.00 123 pp.

CONTENTS

TABLES

XI. Grounds for divorce by state
XII. Grounds for divorce by subject
XIII. Remarriage of divorced spouses

LEGAL RIGHTS OF MARRIED WOMEN, by
Daniel J. deBenedictis

CORNERSTONE LIBRARY
630 FIFTH AVENUE
NEW YORK, NEW YORK 10020
1969, $1.25

CONTENTS

1. Is Your Marriage Legal?
2. Husband's Duty to Support Wife and Children
3. Wife's Responsibilities to Husband and Children
4. Wife's Rights to Property and Income
5. What Are Your Sexual Obligations?
6. A Child's Duty to a Parent
7. Wife's Liabilities to Third Parties
8. How to Protect Yourself in a Real Estate Transaction
9. What You Need to Know About Insurance
10. What You Should Know About Wills
11. Alienation of Affection, Extramarital Relations, Abortions, Illegitimacy, Adoption
12. Grounds for Annulment, Separation, or Divorce
13. What to Do Before Annulment, Separation, or Divorce
14. Best Place to Obtain a Divorce
15. Common Mistakes That Allow Husbands to Win Suits Against Their Wives
16. How to Get More Alimony or Child Support

Daniel J. deBenedictis, *a Bachelor of Science from Temple University, holder of a Masters degree in Education from Boston University and a Bachelor of Laws degree from Northeastern University, is a member of the Massachusetts Bar and the Boston Bar Association, and has written many books on law and real estate.*

As a former law professor and real estate consultant he has been asked to advise wives of their legal rights in numerous marital situations. In this book he covers what he believes are the most important questions he has had to answer through the years-questions that concern even those women whose husbands may have the best intentions.

LEGAL RIGHTS OF WOMEN IN FLORIDA, by Stephen H. Butter

PENINSULAR PRINTING, PUBLISHERS
308 N.W. 27TH AVE.
MIAMI, FLA. 33125
1968, $1.25

There is a constant need for law books. Attorneys and judges require extensive treatises covering the intricacies of legal philosophy and statutory interpretation. These works are voluminous and must be supplemented regularly so that our lawyers and courts are current on the latest legal proclamations. But law is also important to the layman. Most people are not concerned with the technicalities of the law or the legal implications of procedural strategy; but they are nevertheless sincerely concerned with their basic legal rights.

Women comprise a major portion of those persons interested in what their legal position is in different situations. Yet, very few books have been written throughout the country, let alone in Florida, concerning the legal rights of women. Those books that have been written are generally a comparison of one state's law with another, or a statement of general law without reference to a particular state's law or a specific set of facts. "Legal Rights of Women in Florida" deals solely with Florida law and Florida cases. It is specific without being technical and is written in non-legal terms without losing the meaning of the law.

CONTENTS

Stephen H. Butter, *a practicing attorney in the Greater Miami area, is licensed to practice in both the Florida and Federal Courts. Mr. Butter is a member of the American Bar Association and on its Special Committee on Domestic Relations. He also belongs to the Florida Bar Association and is a member of its Committee on Family Law. The function of these committees is to propose laws that are contemporary with the needs of the changing society.*

MAKING THE BEST OF IT: A COMMON-SENSE GUIDE TO NEGOTIATING A DIVORCE, by Newton Frohlich

HARPER & ROW
49 EAST 33RD ST.
NEW YORK, N.Y. 10016
1971, $4.95 132 pp.

Every year more than half a million American couples decide to end their marriages. Each of these million men and women face a process they fear will be costly, acrimonious and destructive of privacy; and they add this fear to the inevitable pain of a failed marriage.

But they are wrong. In this cool book on a heated subject, an experienced lawyer advises men and women contemplating divorce 'how to negotiate rather than litigate their divorces!' By knowing how to bargain over such practical matters as alimony, child support, custody, finances and planning for the future, 'divorce can be a private, rational and inexpensive arrangement.' There are practical sections on: 'how to find the right lawyer, what about fees?, how to use a divorce counselor, how alimony can save a husband money, how a wife can end up in better circumstances if she bargains instead of litigates, how a husband can make a better deal using "fringe benefits," how to provide for children now and in the future, how to plan for the possibility of remarriage.'

An appendix lists the most commonly used grounds for divorce and the residence requirements in all fifty states, Puerto Rico, the Virgin Islands, Canada and Mexico.

Nothing can make divorce painless for the couples who decide to break up each year. But the legal process can be much less frightening if negotiation is understood as the way to a satisfactory and constructive settlement.

CONTENTS

MARRIAGE, DIVORCE & ADOPTION LAWS OF NEW YORK, by Eugene R. Canudo

GOULD PUBLICATIONS
208–01 JAMAICA AVE.
JAMAICA, N.Y. 11428
1971, $4.50 134 pp.

CONTENTS

MARRIAGE-DIVORCE-ANNULMENT, by Samuel Resnicoff

PAGEANT PRESS
101 Fifth Ave.
New York, N.Y. 10003
1968, $4.50 102 pp.

Samuel Resnicoff has filled a long felt want in this book. He has taken a subject which most people shy away from (until they desperately need the knowledge) and given it an interesting and very readable treatment.

Starting with the very human and emotional feeling of the marriage ceremony he describes the symbolism in a charming and simple chapter on the Judaic ceremony. The picture of the bride walking around the groom seven times in the traditional Jewish ceremony testifying that she will surround him with love and devotion—thus making the ring a continual process of daily understanding—is especially touching.

However, Mr. Resnicoff is far from a sentimentalist. The way he faces facts proves that he is a completely practical and pragmatic man. Throughout the book he shows a deep and abiding respect for the union of man and woman with God as the co-partner. Yet he is sadly aware of the pitfalls.

In his choice of case histories of divorce and annulment there is at least, one which almost every couple can identify with and, as he has proved, most of them completely avoidable. The intelligent dry humor in some of the passages emphasizes his points far more than didactic reasoning ever could. Also, his selection of decisions is wisely chosen with an eye on interest as well as precedent and illustration.

This book should be recommended reading for every prospective bride and groom. To be forewarned is to be forearmed. Mr. Resnicoff's counseling is to be heeded. In fact, he makes it crystal clear that the courts should have a counseling service available for every couple who apply for any kind of separation.

Certainly, after it is too late and the union is faced with dissolution, the factual and legal knowledge contained in "Marriage—Divorce—Annulment" is invaluable.

We should like to see every Rabbi, Priest, Minister, Social Worker and Psychologist acquaint himself with the wisdom contained in the book.

Mr. Resnicoff's knowledge of the subject matter is above reproach. He is also the author of "Protecting Your Rights in Civil Service" and "Corners, Commuters' Pinochle."

CONTENTS

MARRIAGE STABILITY, DIVORCE, AND THE LAW, by Max Rheinstein

THE UNIVERSITY OF CHICAGO PRESS
5801 ELLIS AVENUE
CHICAGO, ILLINOIS 60637
THE UNIVERSITY OF CHICAGO PRESS, LTD.
LONDON
1972, 479 pp.

An internationally known professor of comparative law, Max Rheinstein has traveled widely and has studied the legal and social aspects of divorce wherever he went. This book, written in layman's language, is the summation of his findings.

Dr. Rheinstein provides a view of the history and present status of divorce law and marriage stability in a number of contrasting societies, especially Japan, Italy, Sweden, France, the Soviet Union, and the United States. Western society long adhered to the idea that the availability of divorce breeds divorce, and that the way to protect marriage stability is to make divorce difficult to obtain. However, Dr. Rheinstein points out that divorce—the formal restoration of the freedom of marriage—is not identical with marriage breakdown, a factual event, which may or may not be followed by the formal termination of the legal bond of matrimony.

CONTENTS

MARRIAGE: THIS BUSINESS OF LIVING TOGETHER, by Nathaniel Fishman

PERMISSION OF LIVERIGHT PUBLISHERS, NEW YORK

386 PARK AVENUE SOUTH
NEW YORK, N.Y. 10016
368 pp.

It can be said that no one is really happy alone. No matter how we might vary, twist or turn it—marriage, sought after by many and avoided by some, is the foundation of our social system. It is not made in heaven: it is up to us and here are presented actual cases which will not only help you benefit by the experiences of others, but entertain and amuse you no end with the peculiarities encountered by both married and unmarried folks in the courts of this great country.

Questions such as:

Who Owns Love Letters
Who May Marry and Who May Not
Who Owns the Husbands Pay Check
Who Owns the Engagement Ring After Divorce
When Marriage is Annulled Then What
Widows and Remarriage
Marriage Between Relatives

and a thousand others too numerous to list in a brief description are answered in this book.

There is a special section called "Second Marriage" and a unique marriage question-box at the end of the book which answers perplexing questions most likely to confront the average man or woman who is, was or plans to be married.

CONTENTS

9. Limited Divorce and Separation Agreements
10. The Annulment of Marriage
11. The Woes of Divorce
12. Marriage and the Making of a Will
13. The Second Marriage
14. The Marriage Question-Box (115 Perplexing Matrimonial Questions and Answers)

INDEX

Nathaniel Fishman, *a member of the New York Bar, is also author of "Heirs to Your Money and How to Protect Them" and "Married Woman's Bill of Rights."*

MARRIED TODAY, SINGLE TOMORROW: MARRIAGE BREAKUP AND THE LAW, by Kenneth Donelson

DOUBLEDAY
GARDEN CITY, N.Y. 11530
1969, $1.99 paperback

When marriage breakup is inevitable, due to natural causes of human incompatibility, it need not be an endless, confusing and financially devastating process. An understanding of the procedure will do much to smooth the path and enable the participants to make the most of their lawyers' services. This guide, by a noted attorney and his wife, is the result of research into thousands of cases for the purpose of helping the reader recognize and cope with the various problems he will face.

Written in clear, non-technical language, the book considers the three stages of breakup. Part One discusses causative problems including illness, financial difficulties and incompatibility. Part Two covers the actual breakup and such aspects as how to get the most from your attorney's services, costs of divorce, the grounds for divorce and financial advice on property settlements, support of the children and alimony payments. Part Three discusses what happens after the breakup: who cares for the children, how to live economically, how to handle in-laws, what to consider in remarriage.

Much of the Donelsons' advice is directed toward widows and divorcees since they are usually left with the care of the children and often face a more difficult readjustment to single life. However, the book is useful to both men and women for its expert financial and legal advice, for its specific help concerning divided parenthood, and for its encouragement and understanding of the emotional, social and psychological strains of separation.

CONTENTS

Kenneth Donelson *is a lawyer in Sacramento, California. His wife, Irene, serves as a legal researcher and office manager for her husband. They have authored "When You Need A Lawyer," as well as numerous magazine articles, and are popular lecturers on law for laymen.*

MATRIMONIAL ALLOWANCES IN NEW YORK, by Rothenberg.

CENTRAL BOOK COMPANY, INC.
850 DEKALB AVENUE
BROOKLYN, NEW YORK
$35.00

CONTENTS

MUHAMMEDAN LAW OF MARRIAGE AND DIVORCE,
by Ahmed Shukri

A M S PRESS, 1966
56 EAST 13TH ST.
NEW YORK, N.Y. 10003
$9.00 126 pp.

It is a happy augury of our enlarged point of view that we are beginning to try to understand those from whom we differ. This is true especially of Turkey and, in general, of all Muhammedan countries. We, therefore, welcome the study presented here of the Muhammedan laws and customs relating to marriage and divorce. Though not unaffected entirely by earlier and foreign systems of jurisprudence, this portion of Muhammedan law has remained comparatively unaffected by modern European legislation. It has stood as the private concern of Muhammedan states and communities; and we are enabled to obtain here a view of the social development of Islamic society which is either denied us in other fields or is rendered more complicated by diverse influences from the outside. A study like the following has, therefore, a value above and beyond the confines of pure law. Dr. Shukri has not confined himself to one branch of Muhammedan legal law, but has embraced in his presentation the points of view of the chief schools that have had a part in its development.

CONTENTS

PART II—THE MATRIMONIAL RELATION

1. Duties of the Husband
2. Duties of the Wife
3. Marital Authority

PART III—DIVORCE

1. Repudiation by the Husband (Talak)
2. Separation by Mutual Consent (Khul)
3. Dissolution of Marriage by Judicial Decree
   a. Impotence
   b. Li'an or Imprecation
   c. Ila'
   d. Zihar
   e. Failure to Discharge General Marital Obligations
   f. Apostasy

NATIVE DIVORCE COURTS, by H. P. Kloppers

JUTA AND COMPANY, LTD.
P.O. BOX 30
CAPE TOWN, SOUTH AFRICA
1955, $7.50 103 pp.

Mr. Kloppers "assumed duty in the post of Registrar in 1948 and soon became aware that the procedure in the Native divorce courts was adapted to suit the special circumstances connected with Natives." This gave him the "idea of keeping a 'Black Book' and noting all the peculiarities of this type of work. From this stage it was an easy step to compile this little publication in the hope that it will be of some guidance to practitioners, students and officers of the courts."

CONTENTS

THE NEW CALIFORNIA DIVORCE LAW, by Walter T. Winter

SHERIDAN PUBLICATIONS
110 SUTTER STREET
SAN FRANCISCO, CALIFORNIA 94104
1969

California's new divorce law goes into effect January 1, 1970. The prior law was enacted in 1872. While changes have been made in every regular legislative session since then, the basic concepts on which the old law was founded remained unchanged for nearly a century.

The new law operates on an entirely new concept, one that attempts to eliminate fault or blame from divorce proceedings. There is no law like it in the country, and our sister states will undoubtedly watch the results of this effort with great interest. If it is successful, we can expect other states to pattern new legislation after our law.

CONTENTS

Walter T. Winter, *a native of Germany, came to the United States in 1939. A graduate of the City College of San Francisco and the Golden Gate College School of Law, he has practiced as a specialist in domestic relations law since 1957. He is a member of the State Bar of California, San Francisco Bar Association, and the Domestic Relations Committee of the San Francisco Lawyer's Club. He is also a past-president of the California Chapter of the American Academy of Matrimonial Lawyers.*

THE NEW DIVORCE LAWS CONSOLIDATED, by George G. Brown

SHAW AND SONS, LTD.
SHAWAY HOUSE
LOWER SYDENHAM, SE26 England
1970, £2.40

The aim of this book is to present in one compact volume the new laws relating to Divorce and Matrimonial Proceedings, which for the most part come into operation on January 1, 1971; and in particular,

to Introduce,
to provide a Commentary on, and
to Consolidate

the new laws.

Consolidation of the new laws is necessary because, as the Law Commission says (Law Com. 25), the Matrimonial Proceedings and Property Act "will involve the repeal or amendment of most of the sections in part II and IIII of the Matrimonial Causes Act 1965 . . . and once the Divorce Reform Bill is enacted, it will be gravely out of date since Part I will be copiously amended thereby-and amended in a way which could not be accomplished by textual amendments. We intend to see that preparation of a new consolidation, totally replacing the 1965 Act, is undertaken as soon as possible. This, however, must await our Report on Jurisdiction (a Working Paper on this subject will be circulated for consultation in the near future and on Nullity). It should then be possible to produce a modernised and reasonably comprehensive Matrimonial Causes Act as a step towards the codification of Family Law which is an ultimate objective."

CONTENTS

PASSINGHAM ON THE MATRIMONIAL PROCEEDINGS AND PROPERTY ACT 1970, by Bernard Passingham

BUTTERWORTH & COMPANY
88 KINGSWAY
LONDON WC2B 6AB
ENGLAND
1970, $8.47

The Matrimonial Proceedings and Property Act 1970, which complements the Divorce Reform Act 1969, deals with the financial provision for spouses and children where a marriage has broken down. Both Acts come into force on January 1, 1971. The 1970 Act replaces the existing law, which had been built up over the years in piecemeal fashion and was full of illogical inconsistencies with a comprehensive code relating to ancillary relief and orders, a subject of the greatest importance to practitioners.

CONTENTS

POSTSCRIPT TO MARRIAGE: A PRACTICAL GUIDEBOOK ON DIVORCE, by Charles Rothenberg

CHILTON BOOK COMPANY, 1946.
out of print at this time

Not only is this completely readable book a guide for those who have personal divorce problems, but it is a valuable source of pertinent information for all those interested in the subject of divorce itself: social workers, lawyers, ministers, students of sociology, writers, teachers, and all those laymen with a curiosity about one of the foremost problems of modern society.

CONTENTS

THE PRACTICAL ASPECTS OF DIVORCE PRACTICE, by Herbert Myerberg

THE DAILY RECORD COMPANY, 1961
out of print at this time

This well written and useful book is primarily designed to "point out the pitfalls which confront the practitioner in this branch (divorce) of the law and to suggest the ethical and practical approach to the problems presented." The first edition was based upon a "lecture" delivered by the author under the auspices of the Committee on Continuing Legal Education of the Bar Association of Baltimore City in 1951. It is good to know that a second edition is necessary. One may hope that the third edition when it emerges will contain still more emphasis on the lawyer's responsibility in the first place during the period of domestic strife before the exasperated spouses actually come to the law office set for battle.

CONTENTS

Herbert Myerberg *has been actively engaged in the practice of law since 1932, and is the author of numerous articles published in law journals on a variety of legal subjects, many of which are in the field of Family Law. He has been a member of the faculty of the University of Baltimore since 1934. In 1960, he was appointed by the Court of Appeals of Maryland to its Standing Committee on Rules of Practice and Procedure. As a member of the Governor's Commission on Illegitimacy, Mr. Myerberg has acted as a counsel to the Commission and is presently engaged in drafting a new statute to modernize the "Bastardy Law". In addition to his membership in and work on various committees of the Maryland State and Baltimore City Bar Associations and the American Bar Association, Mr. Myerberg is active in many civic and communal organizations. He is a member of the Board of Directors of the Jewish Big Brother League of Baltimore, having formerly served for eight consecutive years as its President, Big Brothers of America and Canada, and the Baltimore Criminal Justice Commission and the Prisoner's Aid Society.*

PROGRESS IN FAMILY LAW, John S. Bradway—Edited by Richard D. Lambert

AMERICAN ACADEMY OF POLITICAL AND SOCIAL SCIENCE
3937 CHESTNUT STREET
PHILADELPHIA, PA. 19104
1969, $3.00 229 pp.

The present issue of "The Annals" comprises a series of articles discussing recent legal contributions of the field of law to the preventive and remedial solutions which have been built up interprofessionally to deal with modern American family problems. While the legal roots of many of these enterprises lie in the past, we are concerned particularly with what has been happening since about the beginning of the present century. While proponents of these activities find it easy to apply the word "progress" to describe what is going on, no doubt there are others of a less enchanted cast of mind who, more cautiously, prefer to use the word "change." Obviously, those of us who have co-operated in the production of the present volume belong to the "progress" clan. We do not feel that all the problems are solved or that we may sit back complacently and assume that the present impetus will be enough, of itself, to insure continued improvement. But we do feel that we have come a long way and that we are headed in the right direction.

CONTENTS

John S. Bradway, *LL.D., San Diego, California, has been Professor of Law, California Western University, San Diego, since 1965. From 1928 to the present, he has taught law at various colleges and universities including the University of Southern California, Duke University, the University of North Carolina, and Hastings College of Law.*

RAYDEN ON DIVORCE, by Joseph Jackson

BUTTERWORTH & COMPANY
88 KINGSWAY
LONDON WC2B 6AB
ENGLAND
1971, $77.00 300 pp.

The 1971 SUPPLEMENT, which runs to some 300 pages, states the law as of 1st October 1971. It takes account of the latest statutes, rules, regulations and cases. It includes:

- the Guardianship of Minors Act 1971
- the Courts Act 1971
- the Attachment of Earnings Act 1971
- the Nullity of Marriage Act 1971
- the Recognition of Divorces and Legal Separations Act 1971
- the relevant provisions of the Finance Act 1971
- the Legal Aid (General) Regulations 1971
- the Adoption (High Court) Rules 1971
- the Matrimonial Causes Rules 1971
- the Matrimonial Causes (Costs) Rules 1971 and
- the Rules of the Supreme Court (Amendment No. 4) Rules 1971

The cases included in the Supplement are very wide-reaching, dealing with such matters as the retrospective effect of the Matrimonial Proceedings and Property Act 1970, the meaning of the words ". . . the petitioner finds it intolerable to live with the respondent" in section 2 of the Divorce Reform Act, and the approach to costs in consensual divorce cases. The Supplement also includes a Noter-up by means of which the user of the work can see at a glance which pages of the main volume have been affected by the new material.

CONTENTS

CHAPTER

Rayden *has for several decades been the leading work on divorce law, and for this edition its scope has been immensely expanded to include family law in general. The work is a Butterworth Modern Text Book and therefore each edition is kept up to date by the publication, from time to time, of cumulative Supplements. The first Supplement to the Eleventh Edition has just been published to take account of the large number of statutory enactments, rules and regulations in the field of divorce and family law that have come into effect since January, 1971, when the main work was published.*

REES DIVORCE HANDBOOK, by R. F. Yeldham

BUTTERWORTH & COMPANY
88 KINGSWAY
LONDON WC2B 6AB
ENGLAND
1971, $13.86

The book shows how interdependent the workings of these Acts are and how they are likely to work in practice. It deals with the law and practice in operation since 1st January 1971, although brief reference is made where necessary to the situation before that date and the consequence of the changes since that date. As the author states in his Preface, the broad procedural pattern and day to day practice described in this book are likely to remain for some time to come.

CONTENTS

SEPARATION AND DIVORCE, presented by the Joint Committee on Continuing Legal Education of the Virginia Bar Association and Virginia State Bar

THE JOINT COMMITTEE ON CONTINUING LEGAL EDUCATION OF THE VIRGINIA BAR ASSOCIATION
5TH AND FRANKLIN STREET
RICHMOND, VIRGINIA
1971

CONTENTS

THE SEVENTH COMMANDMENT, by T. H. Tracy

ABELARD-SCHUMAN, LTD., 1963
out of print at this time

The rigorous attempts by the courts to deal formally and logically with divorce suits based on the charge of adultery cannot conceal the sad, the comic and the irrational behavior of men and women seeking to loosen their marriage ties.

Here is presented a collection of marital transgressions contested in the courts, a panorama from 1785 to date, of divorce cases in which one or both partners are accused of finding the consolations of marriage beyond its boundaries. The plaintiffs and defendants are from all walks of life, from the rustic to the refined, from the deranged to the dignified. The selected cases are of various kinds, improbable, ironic, sordid and notorious, and all are authentic. The testimony is from tried cases, set forth verbatim, judged by T. H. Tracy to be instructive, and illuminated by this lawyer-author with forensic passion and sardonic wit.

CONTENTS

T. H. Tracy *is a Bostonian by birth. After receiving his law degree from Georgetown Law School, he joined the U. S. Department of Justice and served in the F.B.I. for thirteen years. His first writing effort was naturally, "How to be a G-Man." Mr. Tracy's office is in New York City.*

SHALL I GET A DIVORCE, AND HOW?, by John H. Mariano

COUNCIL ON MARRIAGE RELATIONS, INC., 1946
out of print at this time

CONTENTS

SHYSTERISM, U.S.A., by Charles A. Meeker

B. FOX PUBLISHERS
2605 B VIRGINIA STREET NE
ALBUQUERQUE, NEW MEXICO 87110
1967, $1.00 paperback; $6.00 deluxe

In the book "Shysterism, U.S.A.," Mr. Charles A. Meeker exposes the main practices in our judicial system. For his research, he read and briefed more than 3,000 cases covering all areas of America. This blistering attack is delivered on a no-holds-barred basis. The average trial is cleverly described as "a sublimated brawl with techniques as unscientific as an appendectomy performed with a dull tomahawk in the hands of a Skid-Row bum" who was just recovering from a ten-day drunk.

The author, a graduate of the U.S. Naval Academy, and in law from one of New York's top colleges, states that many of the practices are far more dangerous and frightening than are the exposures made by Jessica Mitford in her censure of "funeral rackets" or those of Mr. Ralph Nader in his denouncments of the automobile manufacturers. He further observes that no citizen is exempt from this piracy, and that Americans are being taken for at least fifty times what the undertakers are clipping them for; and further, that ninety percent of these costs are man-made by the lawyers to fill their pockets with greenbacks.

This according to the author is "the worst criminal fraud & racket ever inflicted on such a vast majority of American citizens by a minority group, and there is a most urgent need for an immediate cleansing."

In this 70,000-word exposé the author observes that many of these practices are deliberate, criminally motivated for enrichment of the "shysters"; that these court swindles are appalling indeed, and that as the state statutes are presently "rigged," the public's hands are tied and they can do little about this outrage.

Mr. Charles A. Meeker is a very destructive critic, resorting to sledge-hammer blows, cold rapier thrusts, jabs and sweeps, and at other times satire to demonstrate his frightful and appalling claims in this very well documented book. He gets in behind the scenes and shows just how these criminal frauds are perfected, while those who are accomplishing it are mouthing claims of fair play and justice.

Included in this exposé are ten proposed Corrective Measures, which if adopted would end this astounding disgrace. This book is further illustrated with 23 caustic cartoons which in themselves tell the complete story. This should be studied and carefully read by every intelligent man and woman in America, for included in the book are hundreds of idea and disclosures that, if studied, could save a family man many times the cost of this book.

CONTENTS

SUBJECT SETS ON LEGAL ADMINISTRATION—MARRIAGE AND DIVORCE (3 volumes). The Irish University Press Series of the British Parliamentary Papers.

IRISH UNIVERSITY PRESS INTERNATIONAL, LTD.
81 MERRION SQUARE
DUBLIN 2 IRELAND

The total cost of this volume set is U.S. $186.00 net. (This price incorporates a 10% discount on the aggregate single volume price.)

One of the important reforms in the British Legal system in the nineteenth century was the removal of litigation dealing with matrimonial problems from the jurisdiction of the Ecclesiastical Courts. Until 1857, when the Matrimonial Causes Court was established, divorce could only be obtained through a private act of Parliament and so was limited to the wealthy. The power of the Ecclesiastical Courts was confined to granting separation orders. The significance of the new divorce court lay in the fact that the middle classes could now obtain divorce. Reforms amending laws dealing with married women's property broke down another barrier in the nineteenth century—until these laws were amended even a woman's earnings belonged to her husband.

MARRIAGE AND DIVORCE VOLUME 1
Reports from Commissioners on the laws of marriage and divorce with minutes of evidence, appendices and indices, 1847–1868, 632 pp. ISBN 7165–0436–7 $76

MARRIAGE AND DIVORCE VOLUME 2
Reports from the select committees on the Married Women's Property Bills England and Scotland, and on nonconformist marriages, with minutes of evidence, appendices and index, 1867–1894, 432 pp. ISBN 7165–0032–9 $52

MARRIAGE AND DIVORCE VOLUME 3
Report from the select committee on marriages in Scotland with other papers and returns relating to marriage and divorce, 1830–1896, 656 pp. ISBN 7165–0037–X $79

TOLSTOY ON DIVORCE, by D. Tolstoy and C. Kenworthy

SWEET AND MAXWELL LTD.
11 NEW FETTER LANE
LONDON EC4P 4EE
ENGLAND
1971, £3.90 617 pp.

The new edition of "Tolstoy on Divorce" describes the law and practice in divorce and other matrimonial proceedings in the High Court, county courts and magistrates' courts. The law is stated as at the beginning of 1971 and thus includes the Divorce Reform Act of 1969 and other statutes which came into force on the 1st January, as well as the numerous amendments to the Matrimonial Causes Rules.

As with previous editions, "Tolstoy" has been written for law students, particulaly those preparing for the Bar and Solicitors' Final Examinations, and for practitioners other than those specialising in divorce (who are catered for by the large standard works), but including those who deal with matrimonial proceedings in magistrates' courts. The book is divided into three parts: Part I deals with the law applicable in divorce and other matrimonial proceedings in the High Court; Part II, which has been written by Mr. Registrar Kenworthy, deals with the practice and procudure in such proceedings; Part III deals with matrimonial proceedings and proceedings with regard to children in the magistrates' courts and on appeal therefrom. There are also Appendices containing the relevant Statutes and rules.

CONTENTS

THE TRUTH ABOUT DIVORCE, by Morris Ploscowe

Reprinted by permission of HAWTHORN BOOKS, INC., 1955
out of print at this time

This is a frank and authoritative book—written in simple language for the lay reader—for anyone considering annulment, separation or divorce. It is also valuable to those who, because of professional or personal relationships, need to be informed about the legal aspects of these questions.

In the United States, the laws affecting marriage and divorce differ from state to state—and the territories and other Federal jurisdictions have their own laws. It is very easy for the average citizen, with a personal problem involving annulment, separation, divorce, alimony, income tax deductions, custody of children or remarriage, to become confused and lost in a maze of questions as he receives advice from a variety of sources. If he decides to do something about his problem, he goes to a lawyer, as he should, for advice.

The purpose of this book is to help that average citizen and his lawyer arrive at a better mutual understanding. Reading this book, the lay person is able to see and to understand just what his legal rights and duties are, what the possibilities for a quick solution to his problems are, and what difficulties he faces. The information given includes not only every state of the Union but territories (such as the Virgin Islands) and certain foreign countries (such as Mexico) as well. A special appendix groups all the basic information by state and territory and another appendix is devoted to income tax problems.

For the lawyer, complete footnote references to case material and legal sources are provided for in a special section at the end of the book. An the case histories included in the body of the book itself make fascinating reading for both layman and lawyer.

CONTENTS

"The Truth About Divorce" is required reading for anyone concerned, personally or professionally, with the problems it discusses. Written by a former New York City magistrate with extensive experience in private practice handling a wide variety of cases involving family matters, it is authoritative and complete. Judge Ploscowe*'s experience as a professor of law and a frequent contributor to both popular and professional periodicals has helped him make it understandable for any intelligent reader. "The Truth About Divorce" will be welcomed by troubled men and women everywhere and by those who must advise them.*

WIVES' LEGAL RIGHTS, by Richard T. Gallen

DELL PUBLISHING COMPANY
750 THIRD AVENUE
NEW YORK, N. Y. 10017
1967, 25¢

Marriage is an emotional relationship, but it is also a legal arrangement: a valid contract between a man and a woman, granting certain rights to each, demanding certain responsibilities of each. In this chapter are answers to the questions wives most often ask about marital rights and obligations. These answers are of a general nature, applicable to most couples, but somewhat flexible from state to state, and in specific cases.

CONTENTS

YOUR MARRIAGE AND THE LAW, by Harriet F. Pilpel and Theodora Zavin

COLLIER BOOKS
866 THIRD AVE
NEW YORK, N. Y. 10020
1964, 95¢ 352 pp.

Families can find themselves in the most tangled situations simply by not being aware of what the law says they can or cannot do. This book shows how the law deals with the various aspects of married life, and how proper legal advice can help avoid heartbreak and expense. It contains frequent references to actual cases from many state courts and discusses clearly and authoritatively such situations as the engagement, getting married, parents' responsibilities to children, adoption, personal and property rights of husbands and wives, birth control, separation, annulments and divorce.

CONTENTS

Harriet F. Pilpel *is a partner in a New York law firm.* Theodora Zavin *is Vice President of Broadcast Music Inc.*

RELIGIOUS ASPECTS OF DIVORCE

CATHOLICS AND DIVORCE, edited by Patrick J. O'Mahony

THOMAS NELSON AND SONS, LTD., 1958
out of print at this time

It is the aim of this book to explain clearly and concisely the Catholic viewpoint on marriage and divorce. It deals with the many aspects of marriage which are widely discussed today—marriage as a lasting union and sacrament, divorce as a social evil, the exclusive power of the Roman Catholic Church over the bond of marriage, and the attitude of the Church towards nullity.

This book is unique in being a number of essays, written by different authorities, linked together into a most valuable treatise. The list of contributors includes such eminent names as Dr. J. C. Heenan, Archbishop of Liverpool, well-known on radio and television, and the Rt. Rev. George A. Beck, Bishop of Salford, prominent for his work in connection with Catholic education in England.

The editor has been a member of the Ecclesiastical Tribunal for a number of years and during that time has lectured on marriage to many audiences both Catholic and non-Catholic. This book has been edited, therefore, after ten years of defending and expounding the Catholic attitude and with full awareness of the many questions likely to arise in the mind of the reader.

'I am confident,' writes the Rev. Joseph Gray, Chancellor of the Archdiocese of Birmingham, 'that this book, simply yet attractively written, will be of great value, not only to scholars but to all who conscientiously seek the truth about marriage.'

CONTENTS

5. DIVORCE TODAY, by John Carmel Heenan-Archbishop of Liverpool

PART THREE

6. THE POWER OF THE CHURCH, by L.L. McReavy-Professor of Moral Theology, Ushaw College.
7. THE CHURCH AND NULLITY OF MARRIAGE, by John Humphreys-Vice Officialis Matrimonial Tribunal, Archdiocese of Birmingham.

APPENDIX: A Comparison of Figures, by Patrick J. O'Mahony

DIVORCE, by Mr. Loraine Boettner

LORAINE BOETTNER, 1960
REPRINTED 1970 BY: SAN FRANCISCO BAPTIST
THEOLOGICAL SEMINARY, SAN FRANCISCO, CALIFORNIA
AVAILABLE FROM THE AUTHOR AT 50¢ POSTPAID:
MR. LORAINE BOETTNER
ROCK PORT, MISSOURI 64482
65¢ 38 pp.

The subject of divorce and remarriage is a very difficult and complicated one, made so in part because of the great variety of human situations involved, but primarily so because the Scriptures bearing on this subject are not always as definite and clear-cut as we might like. Precisely what is commanded or what is implied in Scripture is in several instances a matter of dispute, not only between church members but also between theologians and even between denominations. The result is that this subject has become one of the seriously controversial issues of our day. Individual opinions tend to be formed, not only on the basis of what the Scriptures say, but also on the basis of past training and personal attitudes, so that some people are much more strict in their views than others. We must, therefore, take care that in any particular case we neither approve nor disapprove without making a careful inquiry into the facts.

CONTENTS

DIVORCE, by John Murray

THE PRESBYTERIAN AND REFORMED PUBLISHING CO., INC.
P.O. BOX 185
NUTLEY, N. J. 07110
1961, $2.00 122 pp.

The question of divorce is one that perennially interests and agitates the church. This is true whether we think of the church in the most restricted sense as the local congregation or whether we think in terms of the church as universal. The faithful pastor of the local church may consider himself happy indeed if he does not find himself embroiled in the complications associated with divorce and marital separations. And when we consider the matter more broadly, we find deep-seated differences of viewpoint and interpretation within the historic branches of the Christian church.

It would be presumptuous to claim that a study such as is now being undertaken will resolve the many difficult questions involved. Nevertheless, a better understanding of the teaching of Scripture may be promoted if the pivotal passages are discussed in correlation with one another and some attempt is made to bring the relevant Biblical data to the forefront for reflection and study.

The cardinal passages of Scripture upon which any treatment of the Biblical teaching must turn are Deuteronomy 24:1–4; Matthew 5:31,32; 19:3–12; Mark 10:2–12; Luke 16:18; I Corinthians 7:15; Romans 7:1–3. Our study will, therefore, be largely occupied with the interpretation of these passages.

CONTENTS

DIVORCE, by Sanford G. Shetler

PARKVIEW PRESS
1066 MT. CLINTON PIKE
HARRISBURG, VA. 22801

There is, in recent years, a trend to "restudy" many of the Biblical teachings with a mind to adapting our doctrines to current cultures. There is a sense in which this must ever be the prerogative of the church under the guidance of the Holy Spirit. The Church must ever maintain a warm and flexible application of Scriptural principles as it grows and expands.

Yet, there is a certain timeless quality to the Word to which the writer Jude alludes when he speaks of contending for "the faith once for all delivered to the saints." There is, as Evans declares, no evolution in Theology—no progressive revelation, but the Gospel, as it has been delivered to us, is to be transmitted, intact, to succeeding generations. There is no place where we can alter principles in an attempt to accommodate the Gospel to the times.

Written by the Holy Spirit, the Word has a perennial quality, anticipating all the needs of man until the end of time. Christianity can in no case ever be regarded as being provincial either in time or place. And illumination is not to be confused with revelation, in the Church's solemn duty of COMMUNICATION.

CONTENTS

PART II

—What Constitutes Divorce?

—A Relative Theology Growing Out of State and National Divorce Laws

PART III

—Conclusion

BIBLIOGRAPHY

DIVORCE AND THE BIBLE, by Donald L. Norbie, M.A.

WALTERICK PUBLISHERS
P.O. BOX 2216
KANSAS CITY, KANSAS
1971, 50¢

The divorce rate continues to mount and the United States is being littered with the wreckage of broken homes. The divorce rate per 1,000 population increased to 2.5 in 1965. Other countries are being plagued by the same problems.

In the midst of the seething currents of modern, permissive thought, the Word of God stands like a rock. God's eternal principles do not change and are for man's good always (Deut. 6:24). True happiness is still to be found when one woman and one man take their marriage vows seriously and live together in love and faithfulness until death parts them.

And yet the Lord is able to heal the ravages of sin. It is the prayer of the author that this book will lead Christians to a better understanding of this problem that devastates so many lives.

CONTENTS

DIVORCE, THE CHURCH AND REMARRIAGE, by James G. Emerson, Jr.

THE WESTMINSTER PRESS
WITHERSPOON BUILDING
PHILADELPHIA, PA. 19107
1961,

This book deals with the recurrent, perplexing question: What about the remarriage of divorced people? The author believes that the answer involves not only the minister but also the particular couple and the denomination as a whole. Our church laws have been inadequate, and ministers have not known how to act. Dr. Emerson shows that the laws of Calvin and the insights of other Reformation leaders were sounder regarding the problem than our present laws and practices.

The positions of four representative denominations are examined in detail—the Episcopalian, the Lutheran, the Methodist, and the Presbyterian—and Dr. Emerson argues persuasively for a more lenient attitude. Basically his argument is this: As in the case of any split in God's creation, divorce ought not to exist, but in actual fact it does exist and has existed throughout history. Marriages die. Moreover, they die spiritually as well as physically. If, therefore, remarriage is permitted upon physical death, as it is, it ought likewise to be permitted upon spiritual death.

Remarriage should not, however, be permitted lightly or indiscriminately. The usual insistence upon a "waiting period" of one year should be replaced by a more truly Christian view of time. Moreover, the minister should convince himself, through whatever number of interviews may be necessary, that the couple are not merely "in love" but that they are prepared to join their lives together in all areas and on the highest spiritual plane so that their union may be a true marriage in the sight of God and a "holy estate" in the eyes of the church.

Specifically, "readiness to marry" on the part of a divorcee may be seen in his ability to experience "realized forgiveness"—that is, not merely to understand the doctrine of God's forgiveness but to know in his heart that God has forgiven him, and to be, as a consequence, a released and integrated person.

CONTENTS

James G. Emerson, Jr., *was born in Palo Alto, California, and grew up in the Congregational Church. After being graduated from Stanford University, he switched to the Presbyterian Church and continued his studies at Princeton Theological Seminary and at the University of Chicago. While at Princeton, Dr. Emerson served on the National Staff of the Interseminary Movement, was a traveling secretary for the S.V.M., and went to Europe in 1948 in connection with the World Council and related conferences. He has held charges in Pennsylvania, Illinois, and New York, and is now pastor of the Westminister Presbyterian Church, Bloomfield, New Jersey.*

DIVORCE AND REMARRIAGE, by Guy Duty

BETHANY FELLOWSHIP
6820 AUTO CLUB ROAD
MINNEAPOLIS, MINN. 55431
1967, $3.50 153 pp.

Few issues among God's people have produced as much confusion as that of divorce and remarriage. In this fresh analysis of the words of Scripture relevant to the subject, Rev. Duty takes tremendous strides toward dispelling this confusion.

The author displays a compassionate concern for those who, because of the stigma in many of our churches regarding divorce and remarriage, are treated as "second class Christians." In so doing—and herein lies the uniqueness of his approach—he in no way compromises the words of Scripture or goes beyond what they declare.

With the conviction that God is not the author of confusion or of injustice, Rev. Duty boldly faces the crucial questions: Is dissolution of marriage apart from death possible? And, if so, is remarriage ever valid in God's sight?

In presenting his views, the author makes abundant use of his knowledge of Greek and his studies of the Old and New Testaments, and each conclusion is tested by the eight universally accepted rules of biblical interpretation.

CONTENTS

APPENDIX
EIGHT RULES OF INTERPRETATION
GENERAL BIBLIOGRAPHY

Rev. Guy Duty *was born in Alexandria, Virginia, March 10, 1907. He was ordained in 1931, and has continued his pastoral and teaching work in Virginia, North Carolina, Maryland, New Jersey and New York. His ministry has found wide acceptance in Churches of many denominations.*

The bible and related sciences have been the study of Rev. Duty's life. His writing is characterized by the clarity of a gifted teacher, the thoroughness of a lawyer, and the vision of a prophet.

Rev. Duty is the author of three other outstanding books—"If Ye Continue," "God's Covenants and Our Times," and "Christ's Coming & the World Church."

DIVORCE AND REMARRIAGE, Towards a new Catholic teaching, by Victor J. Pospishil

HERDER & HERDER
232 MADISON AVE.
NEW YORK, N.Y. 10016
1967, $5.95 217 pp.

"Divorce and Remarriage" advances the first detailed argument by a U.S. canon lawyer for permitting remarriage in the church.

"Father Pospishil believes the church can and should use the same divine authority by which it binds Catholics in marriage to release them from that bond. To support his point, the 56 year old theology professor at New York's Manhattan College carefully challenges the Biblical and doctrinal assumption upon which the church's opposition to remarriage after divorce is based. Jesus's injunction, 'What therefore God has joined together, let no man put asunder,' he argues, is not a law but rather 'an ideal desired by God.' As evidence, he reviews the history of the first Christian millenium in which the Eastern and Western churches allowed men—but not women—to deviate from the ideal.

"After the schism between the Eastern and Western churches in 1053, the latter began to codify church laws and, by the thirteenth century, the tenet of permanent marriage—like the ideal of celibacy—was made mandatory in the Latin church. Still, Pospishil contends, no Pope or Church Council has ever infallibly taught that divorced Catholics may not remarry.

"For the Vienna-born author, who has spent sixteen years as head of the marriage court for the Byzantine Rite Catholic diocese of Philadelphia, the marriage practices of the Eastern Orthodox churches, which separated from Rome, are more faithful to the spirit of the Gospels and the early church fathers than Roman Catholicism. Though the Eastern churches still encourage permanent marriage, they now allow divorce and remarriage for a variety of reasons. The Church of Rome, Father Pospishil concludes, can do no less"—from *Newsweek,* March 6, 1967.

CONTENTS

DIVORCE AND REMARRIAGE IN THE EARLY CHURCH, by Pat E. Harrell

R. B. SWEET COMPANY, INC.
BOX 4055
AUSTIN, TEX. 78751
1967, $4.95 256 pp.; $2.95 paperback

Divorce and remarriage are perennial problems for the church. What exactly should the church's attitude be toward the remarried convert or the divorced church member? And are there any valid grounds for divorce?

Historical perspective is essential in answering these vexing questions. In this book, Dr. Harrell shows that the early church (from the New Testament period to the council of Nicea) allowed divorce and remarriage for two reasons only: adultery, or desertion by a pagan spouse. He demonstrates that in cases of divorced and remarried candidates for baptism, no change in their marital status was required.

Other subjects covered include the sexual morality of the ancient world, celibacy, polygamy, marriage ceremonies, birth control, prostitution, and adultery.

CONTENTS

Dr. Pat E. Harrell *is minister to the Bering Drive Church of Christ in Houston, Texas. He received his undergraduate education at Abilene Christian College and his graduate education at Harvard (S.T.B.) and Boston University (Th.D.). He currently serves on the editorial board of the "Restoration Quarterly" and is editor-publisher of "Kerygma," a quarterly journal for preachers.*

DIVORCE AND REMARRIAGE: WHAT THE CHURCH BELIEVES AND WHY, by Hugh C. Warner

ALLEN & UNWIN, LTD., 1954
out of print at this time

There is uncertainty and confusion in the minds of many people about the Church of England's attitude to divorce and remarriage after divorce. Canon Warner here sets out in a popular form the main historical and theological facts which must be understood if there is to be an intelligent grasp of the Church's views. Sir Alan Herbert has lately voiced some criticisms which Canon Warner incidentally sets out to answer and refute.

He raises the question of the power of the State to dissolve a valid marriage; examines the Biblical teaching about sex and marriage; relates the rise of divorce figures with the effect these have on the climate of opinion influencing everybody; and appeals for a closer understanding between all who value the integrity of family life and the future of the institution of marriage.

CONTENTS

Canon Warner *is Educational Secretary to the Church of England Moral Welfare Council, and was for five years Personal Chaplin to Archbishop William Temple. He was Vicar of Epsom for twelve years and his other activities have involved serving as secretary to the Central Youth Council of the Church of England and as a member of the Executive of the National Marriage Guidance Council. His published books include "Christian Youth Leadership," "The Church in Action," "Christian Sex Education," and "Daily Readings in William Temple."*

DIVORCE AND THE ROMAN DOGMA OF NULLITY, by the Ven. Archdeacon R.H. Charles, D.D., D. Litt., LL.D. of Westminster Abbey

T.&T. CLARK
38 GEORGE STREET
EDINBURGH
EH22LQ
SCOTLAND
1970, £ 0.17½

CONTENTS

DIVORCE—VATICAN STYLE, by Oliver Stewart

THE ATTIC PRESS
BOX 1156
GREENWOOD, SOUTH CAROLINA 29646
1971, $1.50 154 pp.

The Sacred Rota, one of the most secret courts of the world, hears evidence of hundreds of broken marriages every year. But almost nothing is known of its nineteen celibate judges or the often tragic cases which come before it from all over the world to the heart of Rome.

What sort of courts are the Roman Catholic marriage courts? How can marriages be proved Null in a religion which allows no divorce? What are the special rights of the Pope which can "put asunder" a broken marriage?

Oliver Stewart has taken a hard but impartial look at the Roman Catholic marriage complex, weighing its apparent inhumanity against the authority it assumes as God's instrument. He has had the rare experience of visiting this ancient court in Rome and of talking to many celebrities and others who have faced the ordeal of appearing before it.

This book comes at a time when Christians everywhere are weighing the factors brought to light by the recent decision in Italian civil life to allow divorce. It brings a unique focus to bear on one of the world's greatest mystries, the right of Roman Catholics to end unwanted marriages while they are denied divorce.

CONTENTS

Rebels
Why Children Matter
A Gilded Cage
The Critics
Rome Seen, Faith Lost

THE DIVORCED CATHOLIC, by James J. Rue, Ph.D. and Louise Shanahan

PAULIST PRESS
400 SETTE DRIVE
PARAMUS, NEW JERSEY 07652
1972, $1.95 312 pp.

This is a wise and helpful book for Catholics whose marriages have ended in civil divorce or who may be faced with that eventuality. Based on actual cases and conversations, it looks frankly at problems such as loneliness, guilt, faith, church law, new friendships, money and sex. It offers suggestions that will help many Catholics live a constructive and happy life after divorce.

CONTENTS

James J. Rue, Ph.D., *is the general director of the American Institution of Family Relations, the oldest and largest family counseling center in the U.S.. He is also founder and executive director of the Sir Thomas More Marriage and Family Clinics of Southern California and is chairman of the Behavioral Sciences licensing board of the State of California. He has been married 25 years and has eight children.*

Louise Shanahan, *a graduate of Case-Western Reserve University and the University of Southern California, is the author of* The Ups and Downs of Marriage. *She is a regular columinst for* Marriage *magazine and has written for radio and television.*

THE JEWISH LAW OF DIVORCE ACCORDING TO BIBLE AND TALMUD, by David Werner Amram

HERMON PRESS
10 EAST 40TH STREET
NEW YORK, NEW YORK
1968, $5.25 224 pp.

The distinguished nineteenth century legal historian compares the Biblical-Talmudic view with that of the New Testament and Mohammendan law. He also discusses such related subjects as forbidden marriages, the legal and social status of the divorced woman, and her property and custody rights. He gives a step-by-step procedure of the Get as prescribed by the Shulhan Aruk.

CONTENTS

JEWISH MATRIMONIAL LAW IN THE MIDDLE AGES, by Ze'ev W. Falk. SERIES: Scripta Judaica, edited by A. Altmann and J. G. Weiss, Vol. VI.

THE CLARENDON PRESS
84 FIFTH AVE.
NEW YORK, N.Y. 10011
1966, $6.40

CONTENTS

Ze'ev W. Falk, *Senior Lecturer of Jewish Law, Tel Aviv University, is a Fellow of the Hebrew University of Jerusalem.*

JEWS AND DIVORCE, Edited by Dr. Jacob Freid

COMMISSION ON SYNAGOGUE RELATIONS, FEDERATION OF JEWISH PHILANTHROPIES OF NEW YORK 1968
out of print as of October, 1971

CONTENTS

LIVING ALONE, a Guide for the Single Woman, by William B. Faherty, S.J.

C. SHEED AND WARD INC.
64 UNIVERSITY PLACE
NEW YORK, N.Y. 10003
1964, $3.95 155 pp.

Poets, playwrights and many other people have too often looked upon single women in two ways: the single woman is missing out on life's pleasures because she is not married, or else, since she has not won her prince, she must, like star-crossed Spanish princesses, flee posthaste to a convent.

In this study, Father William Faherty, S.J., succeeds in showing that the situation is not so simple and, fortunately, much more hopeful. While the author does not omit completely the possibility of marriage or the religious life, he proves convincingly that the single woman can lead a challenging and rewarding life in the single state. Free of many of the time-consuming obligations of marriage and the convent, the single woman can pursue a life of leisure and culture not always possible to the married and religious. She can thus devote herself to reading, travel, social work, politics, recreation. In all her activity, she can, and does, remain faithful to herself, her family and friends, and her God.

Relying on his experience as a counselor of women and on a survey of women in all careers—executive secretaries, librarians, nurses, teachers, social workers—the author is aware of the problems and challenges of modern women.

To these women he offers practical and even witty guidance. While considering the more serious aspects of women's life, such as her job or her relations with her family, the writer does not neglect the lighter side, such as trips to the Rockies, "Florida parties" in mid-winter, and apartment hunting.

CONTENTS

William B. Faherty, S.J., *served as General Editor of the* Queen's Works *Publications from 1960 to 1962, and is a former Chairman of the Social Action Committee of the National Conference of Sodality Directors. On two separate occasions he has won Fiction Awards from the Catholic Press Association.*

Born in St. Louis in 1914, Father Faherty attended St. Louis University, receiving his doctor's degree in 1949. He is currently a member of the History Department of St. Louis University and is engaged in research on the history of that institution. He is also a member of the staff of the Sacred Heart Radio and TV Program.

Classifying himself as "not an expert, but a good intermediate skier," Father Faherty also admits to having climbed several of Colorado's highest mountain peaks. His continuing interest in Papal Teaching on Social Issues (with special emphasis on woman's role in modern life) has been expressed in frequent contributions to such magazines as America Today, Homiletic and Pastoral Review, *and* Pastoral Life.

MARRIAGE BREAKDOWN, DIVORCE, REMARRIAGE: A CHRISTIAN UNDERSTANDING; THE SECOND AND FINAL REPORT, by The United Church of Canada Commission on Christian Marriage and Divorce

BOARD OF CHRISTIAN EDUCATION
OF THE UNITED CHURCH OF CANADA
1962, 118 pp.

This Report Number Two surveys the present situation in Canada and makes specific proposals concerning the attitude and responsibility of The United Church of Canada with respect to marriage failure, divorce, remarriage of divorced persons and related matters.

In accordance with the instructions of the Twentieth General Council, meeting in London, Ontario, September 1962, this Report and Record of the Actions taken by the General Council is published for consideration by ministers, church officials, groups of young people and adults, presbyteries and other interested persons.

Report Number One, submitted to the Nineteenth General Council in 1960, set forth a Christian understanding of sex, love, marriage and family responsibilities. This report was given general approval by the General Council. Its recommendations, with some amendment, were adopted.

CONTENTS

MARRIAGE, DIVORCE AND REMARRIAGE, by Ray H. Lanier

LAMBERT BOOK HOUSE
133 KINGS HIGHWAY BOX 4007
SHREVEPORT, LA. 71104
1970, $1.00

Man's happiness on Earth and in Heaven may be determined by the three words of the title of the book.

CONTENTS

MARRIAGE, DIVORCE AND THE CHURCH, The Report of a Commission appointed by the Archbishop of Canterbury to prepare a statement on the Christian Doctrine of Marriage

SOCIETY FOR PROMOTING CHRISTIAN KNOWLEDGE
HOLY TRINITY CHURCH
MARYLEBONE ROAD
LONDON NWI 4DU, ENGLAND
1971, 170 pp.

The conditions of modern life have caused both Church and State to re-examine their attitudes to marriage and divorce. On 1 January 1971 the Divorce Reform Act 1969 came into force-an act under which a concept of the matrimonial offence was abandoned and divorce based solely on the fact of irretrievable breakdown. The Church of England was already engaged in a reappraisal of its own attitude to marriage at the time when the new law first came up for consideration. *Putting Asunder* 91966), the report of a Church of England group on the subject of the secular law, had considerable influence on the framing of the 1969 Act. The Church's discipline with regard to the remarriage of divorced persons had come to be regarded by many as unsatisfactory, and in 1967 the Convocation of Canterbury asked for the whole subject to be examined and for a statement to be prepared on the Christian doctrine of marriage. The commission set up for this purpose by the Archbishop of Canterbury has considered past and present attitudes of the Christian Church to marriage and approaches the problem in terms of personal relationships rather than of theoretical assumptions.

CONTENTS

THE PARTING OF WAYS, by Rabbi Moses Mescheloff (The Fundamentals of Jewish Divorce)

THE CHICAGO RABBINICAL COUNCIL (pamphlet)
SHERMAN HOUSE, CLARK AND RANDOLPH STREETS
CHICAGO, ILL. 60601

When He created the world, God looked "and saw that it was good." Only one condition He declared to be *not good*: "It is not good for man to be alone."

Man and woman were blessed that they "be fruitful and multiply and fill the earth." Married life was to be a union of equals. "I shall make for him," the Lord said, "a helpmate suitable for him." For the Jew the Torah created the climate for man's great happiness, "Shalom Bayis," domestic tranquility.

And yet, this highest state of Jewish blessing can fail. The Torah recognizes that the bonds of matrimony are sometimes to be severed. Where this is necessary, Judaism has established the institution of divorce. The Torah expresses the basic principles which may make divorce advisable or even mandatory. The Talmud lists and discusses many grounds, both for the husband and for the wife, which are sufficient for the granting of a divorce. However, the radical step of divorce is never to be taken lightly.

PROBLEMS OF MARRIAGE AND DIVORCE, by Geoffrey Francis Fisher

MOREHOUSE AND GORHAM CO.
14 EAST 41ST STREET
NEW YORK, NEW YORK 10017
1955, 29 pp.

It should be noted that the Archbishop of Canterbury, in this address, was speaking against the background of the canon law of the Church of England. The canon law of the American Episcopal Church, while generally in accord with that of the Church of England, differs in some particulars, notably in the list of impediments to Christian marriage. The specific laws of the Protestant Episcopal Church in the United States are to be found in Canons 16, 17, and 18 of the Canons of General Conventions.

THE INSTITUTION OF MARRIAGE always has presented, and always will present, vastly complicated and difficult problems to both Church and State, for it involves so many different aspects of human life. It is first of all a deeply personal matter, but at the same time one which closely affects social well-being; it is productive of many moral problems and is involved in many legal complexities; and through it all religious principles of high importance are at stake. Entering so profoundly into the personal, religious, and social life of man, marriage cannot but present problems of acute complexity.

PUTTING ASUNDER, A Divorce Law for Contemporary Society

SOCIETY FOR PROMOTING CHRISTIAN KNOWLEDGE
HOLY TRINITY CHURCH
MARYLEBONE ROAD
LONDON NW1 4DU
ENGLAND
1966, 172 pp.

This volume contains the report of a group appointed by the Archbishop of Canterbury to review the divorce law of England. The Chairman of the group was the Bishop of Exeter, and among the eleven other members have been representatives of theology, the law, social and ethical studies, and psychological medicine. By its terms of reference the group was invited, while recognizing the difference in the attitudes of Church and State to the further marriage of a divorced person whose former partner is still living, to consider whether any new principle or procedure in the law of the State would be likely to operate, first, more justly and with greater assistance to the stability of marriage and the happiness of all concerned, including children; and, secondly, in such a way as to do nothing to undermine the approach of couples to marriage as a life-long covenant. These terms of reference excluded the question of the Church's marriage discipline for its own members; but this Report gives, with full background documentation, the conclusions reached by the group, after considering both oral and written evidence as well as many letters recounting personal experiences, on reform of the divorce law of the State in this second half of the twentieth century.

CONTENTS

A Historical Retrospect: The Attitude of the Church to Civil Divorce Laws

B The Law of Divorce in Some Countries

C Further Observations on the Law and the Courts

D Psychological Considerations

E Matrimonial Reconciliation

F Sociological Considerations, by Professor Donald MacRae

G Evidence Received

WHEN MARRIAGE ENDS, by Russell J. Becker

FORTRESS PRESS
2900 QUEEN LANE
PHILADELPHIA, PA. 19129
1971, $1.50

Post-marital counseling, often neglected, is far more urgent than many suppose. Failure in human relations requires personal reassessment by the involved parties or they risk repeating earlier mistakes. Children are especially vulnerable to bearing the weight of parental failure. Russell Becker outlines some ways to "work through" the emotions that can follow divorce. Those who face the issues of post-divorce counseling will be rewarded with a true emancipation and a new strength for living, says the author. Whether or not the reader has gone to a counselor, he will gain expert assistance from Dr. Becker's practical and case-oriented discussion of divorce.

CONTENTS

Russell J. Becker *is pastor of the Glencoe Union Church in Illinois and the author of "Family Pastoral Care."*

SOCIOLOGICAL ASPECTS OF DIVORCE

AMERICAN MARRIAGE AND DIVORCE, by Dr. Paul H. Jacobson

out of print at this time
available as OP 31,415 from:
UNIVERSITY MICROFILMS
300 N. ZEEB ROAD
ANN ARBOR, MICHIGAN 48106
1959; microfilm price, $12.35

This books deals with the occurrence, duration, and dissolution of marriage in the United States. For the first time, nationwide data are made available on such topics as the chances of marriage and of remarriage, the frequency of religious ceremonies, the duration of marriage and of widowhood, the chances of celebrating wedding anniversaries, the frequency of racial intermarriage, and the probabilities of divorce and of widowhood. Other topics are Gretna Greens, effectiveness of premarital regulations, seasonal pattern of marriage, interval between divorce and remarriage, stability of war and of depression marriages, causes of divorce, children in divorce, orphanhood, divorce proceedings and alimony. Divorce and annulment in South Carolina and New York, and migratory divorce are reviewed in detail. Also highlighted are the changes in trend engendered by the depression of the 1930's and by World War II. Most subjects cover events of the twentieth century; some antedate the Civil War.

CONTENTS

AMERICARERS, A CURE FOR THE CANCER OF DIVORCE, by Grace Curran

CHRISTOPHER PUBLISHING HOUSE
53 BILLINGS ROAD
NORTH QUINCY, MASS. 02171
1968, $3.95 62 pp.

The nature and health of a nation reflects the quality of the people within it: the whole cloth is as fine as the threads of which it is woven. The family, as the basic unit in our society, is deteriorating in alarming proportions. Those proponents of abolishing marriage could profit by the realization that no nation in recorded history has survived without it. Holy matrimony has greatly degenerated into unholy mockery of a once honorable contract.

In the absence of any alternative workable arrangement for men, women and their children to function, it would seem logical to examine the family body, treat it and concentrate on making it sound and whole again. And that is precisely what this book does —examines the problem and presents practical solutions to remedy it.

PART 1. A Diagnosis
2. A Prescription
3. Prevention

The author, Grace Curran, *is well qualified to have written this book. She is a well known lecturer and writer on the family and the many social problems resulting from domestic discord. Some of the more sought after articles she has written are "How a Town Can Unite For Youth," "Good Citizens Are Homemade," "Happiness Redefined," "Divorce Crippler," and "Marry in Haste."*

BACK IN CIRCULATION, by Jean Libman Block

THE MACMILLAN COMPANY
866 THIRD AVE.
NEW YORK, N.Y. 10022
1969, $5.95 285 pp.

You're back in circulation, back again in the world of single people after anywhere from a few weeks to virtually a lifetime of marriage. You're on your own because death, divorce, or separation took your husband from you. You're alone in a sense; but you are not truly alone. You have a great deal of company. You are more than twelve million American women. . . .

Whether young or old, how do you again become a "single woman"? The question obviously is not one but many, and *Back in Circulation* provides the answers. Jean Libman Block begins by discussing the complex emotional reactions that occur whether separation comes by choice or not. She describes the wholly unanticipated sense of loss—instead of unalloved relief—that the divorced woman may experience in addition to a sense of defeat and guilt. She points out the similarities in the reactions of both newly divorced and widowed and tells when friends and family may be helpful and when not. She describes the various stages of grief through which the widow must go, emphasizing that there is no hurrying the total grieving process.

The author then proceeds to all the pratical problems of the woman alone: how to manage your money or to find someone to manage it for you; what legal problems you are likely to face and how to overcome them; how to find a job; how to re-establish your social life; how to take care of yourself after having been looked after; how to cope with your children; how to overcome loneliness; how to meet (and avoid) new men; whether or not to remarry.

In short, *Back in Circulation* tells you how to become a person —possibly quite a different person from the woman you were, but a woman with a strong personal identity and a full life of your own. Based on interviews with lawyers, psychologists, marriage counselors, doctors—and, of course, women themselves, whose thoughts and experiences are given throughout the text—*Back in Circulation* provides clear, comprehensive, sound advice to the woman on her own.

CONTENTS

Jean Libman Block *is a free-lance writer living in New York who contributes regularly to "Good Housekeeping" and "Reader's Digest." Her books include* "There Goes What's Her Name" *(with Virginia Graham) and* "Toujours Forever," *a novel (with Ren Glasser).*

BEFORE DIVORCE, by John Monroe Vayhinger

FORTRESS PRESS
2900 QUEEN LANE
PHILADELPHIA, PA. 19129
1972, $1.50

"Many divorces can be avoided when both parties and a counselor take a second look at the marriage." John Vayhinger speaks to people who are seeking viable solutions to their marital conflicts. For those just drifting along in their marriage, he stresses the importance of moving towards positive attitudes and a better relationship.

Vayhinger discusses marriage—its beginning, growth and common areas of conflict—in a way that will help couples assess their own situation. The author suggests what courses of action are open to a couple and how different decisions affect children.

"Before Divorce" has value for any couple having difficulties, whether or not they are contemplating a legal break. It also makes a valuable addition to the marriage counselor's library.

CONTENTS

John Monroe Vayhinger *is a clinical psychologist in Anderson, Indiana. Along with his practice, he teaches psychology and pastoral care at Anderson School of Theology.*

THE BONDS OF ACRIMONY, by Rose DeWolf

J.B. LIPPINCOTT COMPANY
521 FIFTH AVE.
NEW YORK, N.Y. 10017
1970, $5.95 160 pp.

Divorce can be infuriating, fraudulent, frustrating, and sometimes terribly funny—unless it's happening to you. In this book, Rose DeWolf tells the divorce story law books don't talk about, the story nobody believes can happen—until it does. And the facts are astonishing. *The Bonds of Acrimony* reveals: How you can't get a divorce in most courts unless one side invents degrading lies and the other side goes along with the hoax; the underhanded way husbands and wives snatch and grab for the spoils. *Bonds of Acrimony* pinpoints the surprising profits lawyers make from divorce; how the law turns naturally decent people into conniving opportunists. *Bonds of Acrimony* comments on people who want a divorce and can't get one and people who have grounds for divorce and don't want one. *Bonds of Acrimony* explains why divorce reform is an idea whose time has come and how the laws governing the marriage relationship are changing and why.

But, most of all, here is a book which, in a style that is often breezy and humorous, presents a serious message: Divorce laws, already liberalized in some states, must be changed everywhere so that men, women, and children can be spared the bonds of acrimony.

CONTENTS

Rose DeWolf *was born in Reading, Pennsylvania, and has spent most of her life in the Philadelphia area. A graduate of Temple University, she intended to become a schoolteacher but succumbed to the lure of the newspaper world. She has been a newspaper reporter and columnist for fourteen years, and her column, "Off Center," appears twice a week in the* Philadelphia Bulletin. *Whenever she devotes the column to the problems of people tangled in "the bonds of acrimony," she receives many requests from readers for advice on divorce. Miss DeWolf also has a weekly show on television called "On Camera."*

THE BOYS AND GIRLS BOOK ABOUT DIVORCE: With an Introduction for Parents, by Richard A. Gardner, M.D.

SCIENCE HOUSE, INC.
59 FOURTH AVE.
NEW YORK, N.Y. 10003
1970, $7.95

The Boys and Girls Book About Divorce is the first book on the subject specifically written to be read by children themselves. It was prepared from data collected by the author during thirteen years of therapeutic work with divorced parents and their children. The book discusses the problems usually encountered by such children, and much that is explained to them is applicable to their parents as well.

As Dr. Nathan W. Ackerman, Clinical Professor of Psychiatry, Columbia University, states: "This guide for children of divorced parents, composed by a child psychiatrist, meets an urgent need. These children suffer not only the pains of a broken home, but are, all too often, manipulated, scapegoated and cheated of the truth by parents shamed and defeated by their marital blunder. For this additional assault on the child victims the author offers an antidote, a simple and sincere enlightenment as to the basic human issues of parent-child relations. Dr. Gardner holds an abiding faith in the integrity and basic strength of children, and responds to their anxieties with intelligent, straight-forward, helpful suggestions. He feels that children are not, in fact, so fragile; they are often able to accept the painful realities of a divorce if the adults around them have the courage to be honest. With this stand, I fully concur. It is straight talk, informed, honest; in short, admirably done. The design of the book is enhanced by sensitive drawings which illustrate the basic themes. Children who read this book will feel better about their troubles."

CONTENTS

Richard A. Gardner, M.D., *a child psychiatrist and psychoanalyst, is a member of the faculties of Columbia University, College of Physicians and Surgeons, and the William A. White Psychoanalytic Institute. In addition, he is Associate Attending Psychiatrist at the Presbyterian Hospital in New York City and Assistant Attending Psychiatrist at the New York State Psychiatric Institute.*

Dr. Gardner has published extensively in the fields of child psychiatry and psychoanalysis. He is the author of "The Child's Book About Brain Injury," as well as "Therapeutic Communication With Children: The Mutual Storytelling Technique," which is attracting increasing attention as a valuable therapeutic modality, and was published by Science House in 1971.

CHILDREN OF DIVORCE, by Juliette L. Despert

DOUBLEDAY
GARDEN CITY, N.Y. 11530
1962, $1.45 282 pp.

J. Louise Despert, M.D., a famous child psychiatrist, shows you how to help your children through the special crises and everyday problems of divorce.

CONTENTS

CHILDREN OF DIVORCED COUPLES, by the U.S. Department of Health, Education and Welfare

U.S. DEPARTMENT OF HEALTH, EDUCATION AND WELFARE
PUBLIC HEALTH SERVICE
HEALTH SERVICES AND MENTAL HEALTH ADMINISTRATION
ROCKVILLE, MARYLAND 20852
1970, 50¢

In recent years, over one-half million children have been involved in divorce cases each year, and this number is increasing. The mean number of children per decree increased from 0.78 in 1950 to 1.36 in 1964, but declined to 1.32 in 1965, the first such decline since 1950. The national rate per 1,000 children under 18 years increased from 6.3 in 1950 to 8.9 in 1965. Similar changes were found in the 29 states which reported the statistical information.

The likelihood of divorce was higher for small rather than large families. In the United States, in 1960, the divorce rate was 18.7 per 1,000 couples with no children and 8.9 per 1,000 couples with children under 18 years of age. Among the latter, the rate varied between 11.4 for couples with one child and 6.0 for those with four or more children.

CONTENTS

CHILDREN OF SEPARATION AND DIVORCE, by Irving R. Stuart and Lawrence E. Abt

GROSSMAN PUBLISHERS
625 MADISON AVENUE
NEW YORK, NEW YORK 10022
1972, $12.50

One out of every three American marriages ends in separation or divorce. In 1970, almost three-quarters of a million couples were divorced, and as many as a million children were affected. The consequences of separation and divorce are often severe: a legacy of bitterness between the husband and wife, a shattering of their children's world, legal and religious quarreling, confusion and dislocation of both psychic and social. Yet for all the severity of the problems accompanying separation and divorce, and for all the frequency with which they occur, there has as yet been no book like this one: a collection of articles written by specialists-psychologists, lawyers, clergymen, and social workers—that examine the problems in laymen's language and show how their effects can be minimized or overcome.

CONTENTS

Both the editors of Children of Separation and Divorce *are psychologists, and both earned their doctorates from New York University. Irving R. Stuart has contributed articles to the* Journal of Social Psychology, Journal of Perceptual and Motor Skills, *and* Journal of Aesthetic Education; *he is currently completing a book on interracial marriage. Lawrence E. Abt is the author of* Projective Psychology, Progress in Clinical Psychology *(volumes 1–8), and* Acting Out; *with Stanley Rosner, Dr. Abt edited* The Creative Experience, *published by Grossman in 1970.*

DIVORCE—A STUDY IN SOCIAL CAUSATION—James P. Lichtenberger

originally published by Columbia University Press, 1909
A M S PRESS
56 EAST 13TH ST.
NEW YORK, N.Y. 10003
1968, $12.50 231 pp.

Believing that we could contribute most to the proper understanding of the subject as a whole by an intensive study of some specific field of observation, we have limited our task to an interpretation of the facts exhibited in Continental United States for a period of forty years, 1867–1906, for which the data are most readily accessible.

CONTENTS

The writer of this dissertation was born near Decatur, Illinois, June 10, 1870. He received the degree of A.B. from Eureka College, Eureka, Illinois, in 1893, and entered immediately the Christian ministry in the Church of the Disciples of Christ in his native state. He received the degree of A.M. from Hiram College, Hiram, Ohio, in 1902, after which he held pastorates in Buffalo and in New York City. From 1903 he was a student at the School of Political Science, Columbia University, attending the lectures of Professors Franklin H. Giddings, John B. Clark, and Henry R. Seager, taking work in Philosophy under Professor J. B. Woodbridge, in the Department of Philosophy in Columbia University, and under Professor George Wiliam Knox, in the Union Theological Seminary, and taking part in the Sociological Seminar of Professor Giddings. In 1908, he resigned his New York pastorate and was appointed Lecturer in Political Science, Extension Teaching, in Columbia University, and also Senior Fellow in the Bureau of Social Research of the New York School of Philanthropy. In 1909, he was elected Assistant Professor of Sociology of the University of Pennyslvania.

DIVORCE AND AFTER, Edited by Paul Bohannan

DOUBLEDAY
GARDEN CITY, N.Y. 11530
1970, $6.95 301 pp.; $1.95 paperback

Divorce has changed but we have continued to mouth platitudes that proved unserviceable even in the past. With divorce, an accepted fact in modern life, the number of people involved in a divorce increases—divorcees, new mates of divorcees, children of divorce. In this situation, we must re-evaluate exactly what a divorce is.

A divorce does not end everything about a marriage. It severs the legal contract between husband and wife—but leaves a moral and emotional contract between ex-husband and ex-wife. It shatters the household that was based on the marriage—but it cannot break the relationships that the children of the marriage create merely by existing.

In this book, Paul Bohannan has asked authorities in sociology, anthropology, psychology, medicine and the law to discuss the process and the aftermath of divorce: the divorce process itself; the reactions of friends; the post marital, social, and family relationships; what marriage and divorce mean in other societies (Eskimo, Swedish and Kanuri); the role of the family court; and the prospects for divorce reform.

CONTENTS

Bohannan *is Professor of Anthropology at Northwestern University. He is author of a number of books including* "Love, Sex and Being Human" *and* "Africa and Africans." *He is also co-editor of the journal "American Anthropologist."*

DIVORCE AND THE AMERICAN DIVORCE NOVEL, A STUDY IN LITERATURE REFLECTIONS OF SOCIAL INFLUENCES. 1858–1937., by James H. Barnett © 1939, 1967, New York: Russell and Russell

RUSSELL AND RUSSELL, DIVISION OF ATHENEUM PUBLISHERS
122 EAST 42 STREET
NEW YORK, NEW YORK 10017
reissued 1968

It is not often that doctoral dissertations surmount the circumstances of their origin, so I am very pleased that "DIVORCE AND THE AMERICAN NOVEL, 1858–1937" is being reissued some twenty-nine years after its original publication in 1939. I hope the venture will confirm the judgment of RUSSELL AND RUSSELL, publishers of this reprinting. No doubt, the significance of divorce to contemporary Americans is in part responsible for the persistent concern for a wide range of writings on this topic. In addition this book was a pioneer work in the United States in the elusive field known as "the sociology of literature," and there are many indications of increasing interest in this area of study. In the near future I hope to set forth in professional journals the results of analyzing the American divorce novels which have appeared during the years that have elapsed since the original thesis was published. Taken in conjunction with the present work, this will provide a long-term analysis of the range of variations on one important social theme treated extensively in popular literature.

James H. Barnett is currently Professor of Sociology at the University of Connecticut in Storrs, Connecticut.

CONTENTS

DIVORCE IN ENGLAND, by Oliver R. McGregor

FERNHILL HOUSE AND WILLIAM HEINEMANN, LTD.
303 PARK AVENUE SOUTH
NEW YORK, N.Y. 10010
1957, $4.00 216 pp.

One hundred years of civil divorce . . . and where do we stand now on this fundamental social issue? Is today's divorce rate evidence of moral decay? Are we in danger of social collapse, and is the future well-being of today's children being sacrificed to parental selfishness?

These are very real questions. A Royal Commission reported on these and related issues last year. Already professional criticism has made it clear that its report has done regrettably little to ascertain the primary social facts in this broad field of inquiry and has neglected also the examination of basic historical evidence.

It is more urgent than ever that a cool and scientific analysis of the present position of divorce should be made available, and that it should be informed by a careful historical perspective. This is exactly what Mr. Mcgregor has aimed to do in his centenary study. As a social scientist, he examines the validity of the statistics and other evidence presented to the Royal Commission, and his attitude conflicts sharply with conventional points of view. While he does not neglect the religious and legal considerations of divorce, he sees the problem as an integral part of the whole changing pattern of family life—yesterday and today.

CONTENTS

DIVORCE IN POLAND, by Jan Gorecki (Subtitle: A Contribution to the Sociology of Law)

HUMANITIES PRESS, INC.
SERIES: STUDIES IN THE SOCIAL SCIENCES, 5
303 PARK AVE. SOUTH
NEW YORK, N.Y. 10010
1970, $10.00

The idea of marriage breakdown as ground for divorce has become, in one or another form, a pattern of growing influence in various countries of the western world. In the east of Europe its acceptance has been complete: all the East European lawmakers have introduced complete and permanent breakdown of marriage as an all-embracing ground for divorce, supplemented by compulsory court conciliation. One major limitation is the recrimination rule: the guilty spouse cannot, in principle, secure a divorce unless the innocent partner agrees to it. In introducing this pattern, its initiators sought to achieve three major goals. First, it was to assure a liberal, but not too liberal access to divorce: if a marriage has become a failure, let the spouses be free to dissolve their union, but only when the breakdown is indeed complete and permanent. Second, the court should mediate conflicts between the spouses and—whenever possible bring about a reconciliation. Third, there are important moral and motivational goals inherent in the rule of recrimination.

To investigate whether and to what these purposes are being realized is the main aim of this study. To do this, it was necessary to collect factual data throwing light on the course of the divorce suit, on some antecedents and behind the scenes happenings connected with it, and on some aspects of the situation which emerge after the divorce. Collecting data took place in Poland and entailed attending divorce suits, analyzing court records and statistical data, interviewing judges, barristers, divorced and reconciled persons, and conducting public opinion polls. The collected material yeilds answers, in varying degree, to the questions that were posed. It indicates the value of the court's estimate of degree of breakdown, and of the court-made prediction of permanency of breakdown. It shows the actual results of judicial conciliatory activity. It throws some light on the rule of recrimination as a supposed norm of "socialist morality," and as a supposed deterrent to misbehavior. It also reveals some of its unintended effects: it appears that the recrimination rule, limited by the innocent spouse's consent, encourages base motives for refusal of consent and often results in payments and threats used to obtain consent. On the whole, the collected data—an empirical report on the divorce law in action in an East European country—should make some contribution to the comparative study of living law and may be of use to those concerned with the problem of divorce law reform, in particular, in Western Europe and North America.

CONTENTS

DIVORCE IN THE PROGRESSIVE ERA, by William O'Neill.

YALE UNIVERSITY PRESS
92A YALE STATION
NEW HAVEN, CONN. 06520
1967, $6.50 295 pp.

The first quarter of the twentieth century in America witnessed the transition from a Victorian to a modern system of values. A major aspect of this cultural change was the "revolution in morals" that overturned Victorian conceptions of love, sex, and family life, and resulted in the madcap social escapades and general rebelliousness of the 1920's. This historical case study demonstrates how a jarring change in moral norms is first resisted and then accommodated after the prevailing orthodoxy has been redefined.

Focusing on the period between 1890 and 1920, Mr. O'Neill traces changing American attitudes toward divorce. He finds that the divorce issue formed the leading edge of the revolution in morals, initiating and dramatizing America's painful approach toward a modern conception of social relationships. In Mr. O'Neill's view,divorce was a natural response on the part of American women to the demands made on them by a Victorian culture, demands worsened by the pressures of an industrializing environment.

At one level, Mr. O'Neill's study is an examination of the influence of ideology upon social change; at another, it is a well documented history of the early twentieth century debate over the divorce issue; at still another, a vivid picture of the birth of one familiar aspect of modern America.

Mr. O'Neill is assistant professor of history at the University of Wisconsin.

CONTENTS

DIVORCE IN THE UNITED STATES, by the Sociological Resources for the Social Studies.

ALLYN AND BACON, INC.
470 ATLANTIC AVENUE
BOSTON, MASS. 02210
1972, $2.00 (paperback text edition set of 10—$8.68)

In this episode you have exposure to some of the problems that interest sociologists who study divorce. But divorce is not a subject for study by social scientists alone; it is also of interest to many other people. In one way or another, all of us come in contact with divorce—some of us more directly than others. In spite of the widespread concern about the divorce rate in our society, it is important to remember that, although all married people have probably contemplated divorce at some time or other, only a minority of marriages end in divorce.

To determine why some marriages end in divorce while others do not is a very complicated business. For some groups of people, the likelihood of divorce is predictable on the basis of observable data—these groups have social characteristics associated with either a high or low divorce rate. For individual marriages, however, prediction on the basis of sociological data is not possible—many personality factors are involved in creating a happy, successful marriage in the complex society of the United States.

Finally, to pass judgment on the "goodness" or "badness" of divorce as it affects our society is perhaps an impossible task. The social significance of divorce in our society is not clearly definable in any scientific way. The social order in the United States today is changing, and changing rapidly, and we should expect changes in all patterned ways of doing things, including changes in the way marriages end.

CONTENTS

THE DIVORCE ISSUE AND REFORM IN 19TH CENTURY INDIANA, by Richard Wires

BALL STATE UNIVERSITY
2000 UNIVERSITY AVE.
MUNCIE, INDIANA
1967, 32 pp.

The path to awareness of the circumstances reported in this brief study was indirect. It began with research on the adventurous career of German archaeologist Heinrich Schliemann, famed excavator of the Homeric sites of early Greek civilization, who appeared rather mysteriously in Indiana to secure a divorce in 1869. A quest for the explanation of his action led to both discoveries and difficulties, for the general situation regarding divorce in Indiana became quite obvious, but there was seemingly no available analysis of the exact nature and development of the question. It appeared that the problem merited attention. The first product of subsequent research endeavors was the publication of an article dealing with a limited phase of the controversy. In the present study a more comprehensive treatment of the subject has been attempted. Award of a research grant from Ball State University has helped to make the investigations possible.

Emphasis of approach in this monograph has been placed on the legal and legislative aspects of the divorce issue and reform. No substantial effort has been directed toward analysis of either statistical data or public opinion. The readily obtainable figures do not permit precise or exhaustive study: often the statistics are available only for specified periods of time, rather than in annual computations, and with time segments chosen for different purposes being dissimilar. Under such circumstances it is possible to grasp general patterns only. Thus, the principal reason for presenting such data in the study is to indicate the relative seriousness of the divorce question. Use of public opinion indicators has been restricted to a few references in order to convey the approximate extent and tone of the controversy. The study is, therefore, essentially one centered on legal principles and legislative procedures involved in the process of securing divorce reform.

CONTENTS

THE DIVORCE PROBLEM, by Walter Francis Willcox (A Study in Statistics)

originally published by Columbia University Press, 1891
A M S PRESS
56 EAST 13TH ST.
NEW YORK, N.Y. 10003
1969, $12.50 74 pp.

The final form of this monograph is the result of a conversion. My study of divorce was commenced when fresh from the reading of philosophy in Germany, and a month or more passed in turning the leaves of Trendelenburg, Bluntschli, Stahl, and the whole line of "Naturrecht" theorizers. Nothing was found to shake the conviction with which I started, that the policy of the Catholic church, refusing remarriage in all cases, is the ideal one for a state to adopt. Then I stumbled upon Bertillon's "Etude Demographique du Divorce" and, undeterred by the columns of figures, read and reread it. My eyes were opened and, deserting the high a priori road of laying down what marriage and divorce ought to be, I betook myself to a patient examination of Mr. Wright's Report in the effort to understand what they are. My conclusions are contained in the following pages. In their present form, therefore, they are based on two books; their method is derived from Bertillon, their data from Wright, and a critic must have keen eyes to detect in them any influence of the first six weeks' reading. If a similar revolution should be started in the mind of any reader by the facts here recorded, I shall be most amply repaid.

CONTENTS

DIVORCE STATISTICS ANALYSIS—UNITED STATES, 1964 and 1965, by The U.S. Department of Health, Education and Welfare.

U.S. DEPARTMENT OF HEALTH, EDUCATION AND WELFARE
PUBLIC HEALTH SERVICE
HEALTH SERVICES AND MENTAL HEALTH ADMINISTRATION
ROCKVILLE, MARYLAND 20852
1969, 60¢

In this report an analysis of divorce and annulment totals is presented for the United States, individual States, and standard metropolitan statistical areas, as well as an analysis of the 1964 and 1965 detailed divorce statistics for the twenty-two states included in the divorce-registration area.

The national divorce rate, which showed little variation for more than a decade, has been increasing in recent years, and this increase cannot be completely explained by the growth in the number of young married couples. Simultaneously, the median age at the time of the decree and the median duration of marriage showed a decline. The average number of children reported per decree declined slightly, reflecting the decrease of births in recent years.

CONTENTS

Similar Reports Available: "DIVORCE STATISTICS ANALYSIS—UNITED STATES–1963, *National Center for Health Statistics Series 21, Number 13;* 'DIVORCE STATISTICS ANALYSIS—UNITED STATES–1962, *National Center for Health Statistics Series 21, Number 7, 40¢.*

DIVORCE WON'T HELP, by Edmund Bergler

HARPER & ROW
49 EAST 33RD ST.
NEW YORK, , N.Y. 10016
1970, hard. $4.95, pap. $1.95   240 pp.

A psychiatrist trained in Freud's Vienna shows that divorce is neither glamorous nor a cure for a bad marriage; and that monogamy—contrary to much of present-day opinion—is the normal and healthy state of man. Dr. Bergler shows that unhappy marriage is usually not the cause but only the symptom of the real difficulty—that unless estranged partners understand the unconscious neurotic patterns which set them at odds, any future marriage will involve the same mistakes.

Out of his practice, Dr. Bergler parades a cross-section of the unhappy husbands and wives who have not yet learned that love is a combination of both the tender and sensual elements of man's nature. Here are the "wolves" (inwardly inflated neurotic "sissies") and frigid women who unerringly seek each other out; the coquette, the weeper, the gold digger, the nagging wife, the tightfisted husband, the dissembler, and the schemer. He explains the "hangover after Reno"; the neurotic basis of frigidity, promiscuity, and homosexuality in women; inpotence and Don Juanism in men; defines the minimum requirements for a good wife; explodes the "myth of the superior male"; and discusses the problems of the children of divorce.

The author bases his arguments on the findings of modern psychiatry and buttresses them with clinical evidence. He writes clearly and with the layman always in mind.

CONTENTS

THE DIVORCED MOTHER, by Carol Mindey

McGRAW-HILL
330 WEST 42ND ST.
NEW YORK, N.Y. 10036
1970, $6.95

"Of the 850,000 persons who are divorced every year (and the rate increases as our population increases), 60 percent are parents, which means that this year about a quarter of a million women will face the overwhelming problems of being divorced mothers. The average divorcee is often naive and totally unprepared for what is ahead of her," writes Carol Mindey, herself a divorced mother.

This sound and practical guide for the mother who is undergoing divorce is the result of the author's own need for facts, information, and advice. To help other women who face the same situation, she shares her experiences and relates with candor and good humor what did and did not work for her.

Specific information on the legal and technical aspects of divorce is provided, such as finding a good lawyer, proper conduct during the predivorce period, and how to survive the actual day in court. The author suggests ways to cope with the realities of running a household without a man, operating on a reduced budget, relationships with neighbors and with family and friends, and raising children.

Perhaps the most insidious consequence of divorce is the trauma that follows. Many mothers and their children suffer overwhelming despair, loneliness, and panic in the early weeks; some even contemplate suicide. With understanding and compassion Carol Mindey offers sensible advice on how to overcome the ensuing emotional stresses and strongly urges that the help of a psychotherapist be sought when the problems seem insurmountable.

Finally, from personal experience, Carol Mindey, who has remarried, covers the subject of romance and marriage.

CONTENTS

DIVORCEE A GO-GO, by Elaine Stanton

HOLLOWAY HOUSE PUBLISHING COMPANY
POST OFFICE BOX 69804
LOS ANGELES, CALIFORNIA 90069
1968, 95 Cents 312pp.

CONTENTS

AUTOBIOGRAPHY

Elaine Stanton tells it the way it is after divorce. This is a wildly funny and completely honest account of her life after the final papers were signed.

Elaine is a gusty girl and the bland diet of PTA meetings and night school was just not for her. She decided to be a "swinger." From kook sex ads to the genuine fulfilling affair, she left her inhibitions behind. She proves that a divorcee doesn't have to wilt on the vine. The pitfalls are many but the rewards are worth the risk.

THE DIVORCEE'S HANDBOOK, by Louise Rohner

DOUBLEDAY, 1967
out of print at this time—150 pp.

When there is no way to stay together, there is separation. When there is no way to close the gap, there is a schism. When there is no help, there is a divorce. But then what?

Then . . . the divorcee must help herself. After the judge's voice, the first sound she hears is a chorus of closing doors. The world of married couples no longer wants her. She does not understand or belong in the young single world. She has lost her place—but not, contrary to the belief of many divorcees, her purpose.

Here is the book that will help a woman to find that purpose, beginning from the day she is divorced. Sometimes blunt, sometimes witty, always sensitively written, *The Divorcee's Handbook* mirrors the author's own experience: that it is quite possible for any divorcee to re-establish a marvelous and rewarding life, with or without a new mate.

Though the primary purpose of this handbook is to inspire the divorced woman to build her own life by learning to live as an independent entity, there are answers to a great many problems of home management and community living faced by the divorcee in our couple- oriented society. Separate chapters cover the kinds of men a divorced woman meets, and suggestions are offered for the handling of the divorcee's new social life. The conclusion is the author's open letter to divorced men.

CONTENTS

1. When put asunder
2. Own your own life
3. Make your time count
4. Organization
5. Bless the children
6. Divorce without children
7. What's-his-name?
8. Friends and sub-friends
9. Boys, boobs and bachelors
10. Mama's boyfriend
11. An open letter to divorced men
12. Your second-time-around valentine

Louise Rhoner *is the mother of four children and is a divorcee. Currently involved in the writing of three other books, including one about her children's adventures in Switzerland, Mrs. Rohner is also the west coast representative for an Hawaiin dress firm. She and her family live in Los Angeles.*

EXPLAINING DIVORCE TO CHILDREN, edited by Earl A. Grollman

BEACON PRESS
25 BEACON ST.
BOSTON, MASS. 02108
1969, $5.95 257 pp.

Must children of divorce be psychologically scarred by their parents' separation? Or are there ways that parents can help a child understand the divorce and what it will mean to him?

"Explaining Divorce to Children" is a serious and compassionate attempt to deal with the special problems of divorces that involve children. For parents who are divorcing, for teachers and other professionals who work with children from divorce backgrounds, it contains valuable information, perspective, and guidance. Nine experts on divorce from the fields of sociology, psychiatry, psychology, law, child study, and the three major religions examine from their varying viewpoints the child's fears, his reactions to tensions and unhappiness, and his undermined sense of security.

The authors agree that there are no pat solutions—a divorce necessarily creates unhappiness and upheaval for those who must live through it, and attempts to fool a child by pretense that "nothing is wrong" can result in the magnification of his anxieties and his inability to express them. The contributors point the ways for parents to deal realistically and reassuringly with their children and thereby relieve the strains on their children and on themselves.

The final chapter is a discussion among six teenagers from divorced homes. Answering the question "Would a broken home break you?" they present their own frank feelings and opinions on how well they managed their own adjustments and why.

FACING LIFE ALONE, WHAT WIDOWS AND DIVORCEES SHOULD KNOW, by Marian Champagne

THE BOBBS-MERRILL COMPANY, INC.
out of print as of October, 1971
1964, $6.50

This book was written for women and for husbands who want their wives prepared. It fills a practical and a vital need for widows and divorcees. It is a complete guidebook of practical information for women who for the first time find themselves alone and forced to face the future alone.

CONTENTS:

Marian Champagne, *besides being a lawyer married to a lawyer, knows whereof she writes. She is a graduate of Smith College, a short story writer, and the author of two novels. She is also the mother of two daughters.*

FOR BETTER OR WORSE: A NEW APPROACH TO MARRIAGE AND DIVORCE, by Morris L. Ernst and David Loth

HARPER & ROW
out of print at this time
1952, $3.00

What happens after the divorce?

In this book a famed lawyer and a publicist consider the human and legal problems that beset millions of divorced people. For the first time, divorce is considered in terms of people's future lives. Here are the personal stories of men, women, and children who have actually been through the divorce mill.

The authors are concerned about the people who have or are likely to contribute to the frightening annual divorce toll (800,000 will probably get divorced this year). In Mr. Ernst's practice, the primary aim has been to help clients achieve a workable marriage. And, when adjustment fails, to help them, through divorce, to embark on an intelligently planned second chance. Few people ever consider in the heat of the divorce battle what their futures will bring. They have no guide to tell them, and under the ridiculous divorce system in this country, it is almost impossible for them to secure such guidance.

"For Better or Worse" is such a guide. The authors have prepared it with the help of hundreds of collaborators. These are men, women, and children in the best possible position to know what happens after divorce. In the most intimate detail, they have written out their stories.

They know now, looking back, whether they were right or wrong, and whether or not they would do it again. They have grappled with problems of money, children, loneliness, friends and families, sex, alcohol, and their own personalities. They share with the reader what they have learned.

Valuable as it is for these revelations, "For Better or Worse" has an even more important purpose. The last chapter offers a program for revamping our divorce procedure. The authors point the way toward the acceptance of more responsibility by the courts through expert personal counseling rather than impersonal judgments handed down on the basis of artificial evidence. The authors clearly demonstrate that children are the most important people in the divorce. The plan is one based on human needs rather than outworn legalisms.

CONTENTS

Mr. Ernst and Mr. Loth *are co-authors of two highly successful books:* American Sexual Behavior and the Kinsey Report *and* the People Know Best.

HOW TO AVOID ALIMONY: A SURVIVAL KIT FOR HUSBANDS, by John S. Rodell

STEIN AND DAY
7 EAST 48TH ST.
NEW YORK, N.Y. 10017
1969, $4.95
Available in Paperback from
Pocket Books Publishers
Division of Simon & Shuster, Inc.
630 Fifth Ave., N.Y., N.Y. 10020
95¢

This disarming but devastating book offers a completely fresh approach to a subject which is usually submerged in sociological cliches and grim legal treatises.

The author, impatiently throwing off the usual helpless attitudes toward the divorce courts and their perpetuation of inequities, zeroes in on the most flagrant absurdity of all: the Wronged Woman's divine right to blackmail and pauperize the man who leaves her.

"How to Avoid Alimony" is not a legal guidebook, but a highly personal and often hilarious account of two divorce proceedings, which the author uses to illuminate the nature of all contested divorces in America. With irreverent wit and undisguised anger, he lets us follow the sneak attack on the unsuspecting husband, his legal sandbagging, the way the courts and even his own lawyer gang up on him.

Interspersed throughout this black farce of twentieth-century American justice are many lessons to help the reader avoid the pitfalls that await him in similar situations. Although the cards are inevitably stacked against the husband, the author has a few tricks up his sleeve that can give any man determined to use them a fair chance of coming out even. The "lessons" consist of errors to avoid as well as positive steps to take, and they are clearly pointed out all along the way. The climactic trick that turns the tide in favor of the husband at the end is a real shocker.

John S. Rodell *is a former advertising copywriter, playwright, and screenwriter who considers himself a veteran of divorce: he has survived three without paying alimony. He lives in Virginia with his fourth wife, a research psychologist at Hollins College, and one son.*

HOW TO BE HAPPILY DIVORCED, by John A. Ross

EXPOSITION-BANNER BOOKS
50 JERICHO TURNPIKE
JERICHO, N.Y. 11753
1968, $5.00 150 pp.
Division of Coronet, Inc.
A Warners Communication Co.
315 Park Ave. South
New York, New York 10010

Being divorced is like being single-almost. And being single is like riding a bicycle: you never really forget how—you only lose the knack. (Especially if you've been married for some time).

Practice, they say, makes perfect. By playing your bachelor cards right, you can have the winning hand in dealing with the ladies (see Chapter 9). No matter what happens, bachelordom revisited can be fun. The proof is amply demonstrated in this delightful refresher course by John A. Ross.

From courtroom (see Chapter 2) to bedroom (see Chapter 9 again), "How to Be Happily Divorced" is a wise and winning guide. It tells the lucky loser how to make his wife's lawyer love him, get the most from his married friends, meet and promote new women; where to take them after he has met them; and, most important, what to do with the girls after he has them (see Chapter 9 again).

Since first dates have always been a trial (see the Book of Genesis, Chapter 3), John Ross has wisely included a chapter on this subject for the eager stag no longer at bay.

"How to Be Happily Divorced" is somewhat of a survival kit. How to avoid costly mistakes in setting up housekeeping, how to cook for both survival and effect, and how to have hobbies with and without sex, are among the problems for which Mr. Ross has the answers.

This is a humorous examination of the sort of life every potential alimony-payer (and one out of every three married men is) may expect and/or hope to lead. Indispensable to the divorced, again-single male, one hesitates to call "How to Be Happily Divorced" a companion piece to Sex and the Single Girl, although the gals will benefit from reading "How to Be Happily Divorced." After all, a divorced man who has learned to live happily often makes a better (perish the thought) husband . . . the next time around.

CONTENTS

John A. Ross *is an attorney, C.P.A., and an investor and inventor as well. He achieved "The impossible dream" of retirement before age forty and has found the ways of enjoying it. Far from being idle, he now has time to read, breathe, travel and tinker with sports cars. He enjoys life sans pills, sans doctors, sans psychiatrists, sans ulcers . . . and he has had the time and zest for living to do the research for this book. Like Mr. Ross says, "The research wasn't too exhausting."*

P.S. Mr. Ross is divorced! (Correction: Mr. Ross is happily divorced!*)*

HOW TO CATCH A MAN, HOW TO KEEP A MAN, HOW TO GET RID OF A MAN, by Zsa Zsa Gabor

DOUBLEDAY
GARDEN CITY, N.Y. 11530
1970, $4.50

To quote Miss Gabor, "Women always ask me for advice about men and love. They think that I must know, because I have such a very bad reputation—and believe me, it's a hard reputation to live up to. The truth is that I am probably more naive than you think. A woman who has almost always been married since she was fifteen and a half years old has lived a much more sheltered life than a girl who was on the loose until she was twenty or twenty-five. But since I have been married so many times and have a wide experience in that, you may learn something from me. I hope you can use my advice. I certainly can't use it myself. I'll always keep making my same mistakes over and over.

"Another problem you'll have when you read my advice is that you may get mixed up, because it's not always logical and consistent. Don't worry though. Advice that's not logical and not consistent is the very best kind. If you don't like what I tell you to do in one place, just keep reading and in a few pages I'll probably tell you to do something different that you'll like a lot better."

CONTENTS

INCREASES IN DIVORCE, by the U.S. Department of Health, Education and Welfare.

U.S. DEPARTMENT OF HEALTH, EDUCATION AND WELFARE
PUBLIC HEALTH SERVICE
HEALTH SERVICES AND MENTAL HEALTH ADMINISTRATION
ROCKVILLE, MARYLAND 20852
1970, 30 cents

In this report are described the increases in the number of divorces and annulments that have occurred in the United States. The national divorce total grew from 428,000 in 1963 to 523,000 in 1967, a 22% increase in four years. Divorces were up much more than could be accounted for by changes in numbers of the married population and its age composition. In recent years, only about one-fourth of the total increase can be explained by changes in the population. Divorces increased in the great majority of states. Since 1963 they have increased not only in the United States but also in most foreign countries.

The divorce rate for the states included in the divorce-registration area is negatively associated with median duration of marriages at decree: States that have a high median duration tend to have low rates and vice versa.

CONTENTS

LOVE, MARRIAGE, AND DIVORCE AND THE SOVEREIGNTY OF THE INDIVIDUAL, by Henry James, Horace Greeley, and Stephen Pearl Andrews.

SOURCE BOOK PRESS
185 MADISON AVENUE
NEW YORK, NEW YORK 10016
1972, 192pp.

As Mr. Andrews aptly states, "The columns of the New York Tribune have been abruptly, though not altogether unexpectedly, close to me, in the midst of a Discussion upon the subjects named in the title-page to this pamphlet, which had been courted and invited by Mr. Horace Greeley, the responsible editor of that influential journal. After detaining my replies to himself and to Mr. James from four to eight weeks, Mr. Greeley at length returns them to me, accompanied by a private note, approving my criticisms upon Mr. James, but assigning reasons for the declination of both of my communications.

"The ostensible grounds for excluding my comments upon positions assumed, and argument in support of those positions, are, 1st. That my replies 'do not get the discussion one inch ahead.' I obviously could not put the discussion ahead by stating and developing new positions, until I had answered those assumed by my opponent. Whether the real reason for 'burking' my rejoinder was that I did not do the last well enough, or that I did it rather too effectively and conclusively for my continued popularity at the Tribune office, so many readers as I shall now be able to reach with some little industry on my part, will have the opportunity to decide. 2nd. That expressions are employed by me which are offensive to the public sense of decency, and especially that the medical illustration of my lady correspondent is unfit for publication. I propose now to publish the rejected replies as written, that the world may judge whether any thing I have said or embodied in them is of a nature which might reasonably be supposed likely to 'dash the modesty' of Mr. Greeley, or the habitual readers of the Tribune."

CONTENTS

LOVE THE SECOND TIME AROUND, by Dorothy M. Freda

LADDIN PRESS
119 EAST 30TH STREET
NEW YORK, N.Y. 10016
1969, $5.95   183 pp.
75 cents from Popular Library
355 Lexington Ave
New York, N.Y. 10017

If you've been widowed or divorced, this is your Bible, the kind of book that will gently, positively and honestly show you how to start living again, laughing again and most important, loving again. It won't be easy—because the shock of suddenly finding yourself alone and lonely in a strange new world may leave scars. To help you erase those scars, Dorothy Marie Freda, a young widow with spirit and spunk, has written this brilliant, compassionate guide for the single-again woman.

Miss Freda proves that love the second time around can be an exciting and challenging experience—and she does more than just tell you . . . she shows you.

The girl who has never married will also find a bonanza of useful suggestions here since she, like the formerly-married woman, has often suffered rejection, doubt, and fear of the future.

Above all, "Love The Second Time Around" is a positive, rewarding reading experience . . . the "must" book for every formerly-married woman who longs to love again.

CONTENTS

Dorothy Marie Freda *is one gal who didn't crawl into a shell when she was widowed in her thirties. Finding herself with two kids to bring up, a minute savings account and a house that was falling apart, she quickly shook off the numbness of widowhood and decided that life still had a great deal to offer—especially to those who were willing to take the initiative. Most important, she started dating again and began to live and enjoy an exciting new life. Because Dorothy Freda never stopped believing that she could, she did.*

A MANUAL ON MARITAL RECONCILIATIONS, by
Lester C. Kohut

FAMILY LAW PUBLICATIONS
P.O. BOX 2192
MADISON, WISC. 53701
1964, $2.85 $1.75 paperback

The author of this provocative book challenges the too-readily believed assumption and assertion that a marriage is dead or broken just because there are grounds for a divorce, because the couple have seemingly "given up," or because some less-than-adequately-skilled person has tried and failed to reconcile the parties. There are strong indications from the author's socio-legal test of his hypothesis that courts, various professions, and society by and large exert something less than an adequate attempt and something less than a modicum of concern in helping distressed couples.

"A Manual on Marital Reconciliations" is an attempt to formulate some standards for ensuring that unbroken marriages do not end up in divorce court. It is an attempt to devise some twentieth century methods for twentieth century problems in family living.

Read about proposed legislation to forestall short duration marriages, about the proposed family court made up of a panel of experts rather than a one-man jury to decide if a marriage is irreparable, about making limited divorce and separation agreements into therapeutic instruments, etc.

No one who reads "A Manual on Marital Reconciliations" will fail to recognize the immensity of the work undone in the area of marital rehabilitation. This book is both unique and challenging and therefore deserves to be widely read.

CONTENTS

9. Some Constructive Proposals Toward a Therapeutic Family Law
10. Epilogue

Lester C. Kohut *is a marriage counselor presently associated with the Family Court of Cook County in Chicago. Apart from his law office experience he has experience in counseling families, alcoholics, and juvenile delinquents.*

MARITAL BREAKDOWN, by Jacob Dominian

PENGUIN BOOKS
7110 AMBASSADOR ROAD
BALTIMORE, MARYLAND 21207
1968, $1.25 172 pp.

The scientific study of marriage began at the turn of the century and has been gathering momentum with each succeeding decade. The United States has taken a lead in this research first through sociology and later with a psychological approach. This book gives a selected survey of this research both in the United States and Britain, to which I have added my own observations, based on ten years' work in this field. Research into marriage is difficult, not only by virtue of the complexity of the subject itself, but because matrimony stands at the centre of powerful social, religious and legal ordinances which influence this most intimate of personal relationships in different ways.

However daunting the difficulties may appear, there is an urgent need to overcome them, for the plight of marriage concerns everyone, the sufferers, their off-spring, and society as a whole. Different religious and ethical backgrounds may divide men and women in the proposed solutions *after* a marriage breaks down, but there is little disagreement about the desirability of identifying the causes *before* this happens.

CONTENTS

Jack Dominian *is head of the Department of Psychological Medicine at the Central Middlesex Hospital; he is also consultant psychiatrist at Shenley Hospital. Since 1958 he has been a medical adviser to the Catholic Marriage Advisory Council particularly concerned with the challenge that modern psychiatry and psychology present to traditional Christian thinking.*

His published investigations cover a wide range of psychiatric subjects, and he has written many articles. He is also the author of "Psychiatry and the Children" (1962) and "Christian Marriage and the Challenge of Change" (1967).

Dr. Dominian is married and has four children.

MARITAL THERAPY: MORAL, SOCIOLOGICAL AND PSYCHOLOGICAL FACTORS, Compiled and Edited by Hirsch Lazaar Silverman

CHARLES C. THOMAS
301–327 EAST LAWRENCE AVE.
SPRINGFIELD, ILL. 62703
1972

Presented by forty-seven nationally known authorities in their respective fields, this comprehensive volume is concerned with the development of marital therapy, especially in the United States, its present status and significant trends that are already manifesting themselves to the point of reshaping the field. Consideration is also given to those significant innovations that are influencing constructive thought in marriage counseling.

The chapters are different in length, format, and emphasis—adding flavor to the volume and making it more readable, challenging, and provocative. Presented in four major sections, the text thoroughly covers:

Psychological Factors
Sociological Factors
Moral Factors
Comprehensive Evaluation: Marital Therapy Concepts

CONTRIBUTORS:

Wesley J. Adams
Gerald Albert
Ben N. Ard, Jr.
Panos D. Bardis
Rev. James R. Becherer
Mary S. Calderone
William Langley Carrington
LeMon Clark
John W. Crandall
William F. Eastman
Albert Ellis
David Goodman
Robert J. Goodstein
Rev. Matti Joensuu
Merle R. Jordan
David O. Moberg
Donald D. Moore
Ethel M. Nash
A. E. Keir Nash
Stephen Neiger
Msgr. John J. O'Sullivan
Lloyd G. Phillips
John G. Quesnell
Clifford B. Reifler
Ira L. Reiss
Isadore Rubin
Charity Eva Runden
Tatsuo Samejimi
Gerald Sanctuary
Rev. Frank A. Sargent, Jr.

Sr. M. Catherine deRicci Killeen
Joseph C. Landrud
Ruth Leder
Eugene B. Linton
David R. Mace
Rev. Paul Marx
Donald J. McCulloch
Thomas G. McGinnis
John O. Meany
Patricia Schiller
Emanuel K. Schwartz
John Seymour
Alfred Stern
Joseph B. Trainer
Rev. Ace L. Tubbs
Rev. Alfred Vail
Leland Foster Wood

Hirsch Lazaar Silverman, Ph.D., Sc.D., L.H.D., LL.D.
Seton Hall University
Graduate Division, School of Education
South Orange, New Jersey
Past President, Academy of Psychologists in Marital Therapy
Past President, New Jersey Association of Marriage Counselors
Chairman, New Jersey State Board of Marriage Counselor Examiners

MARRIAGE AND DIVORCE, by Christopher Macy

PEMBERTON PUBLISHING COMPANY
88 ISLING HIGH STREET
LONDON N1 8EN
ENGLAND
1969, £ 0.47½ 127 pp.

Nine out of ten people who get married stay married. Not all of their marriages are perfect, but they do not break down. A married lifetime today is twice as long as it was in Victorian times, for people are marrying younger and living longer. Even so, young couples are still getting married with the intention of staying married for life. Unless social habits change radically most of them will, though for marriages contracted below the age of twenty the divorce rate is three times the norm.

It is none the less true that marriage is under greater strain than it was. Sexual morality is less restrictive. Less social stigma is now attached to divorce. Legal aid helps to make divorce more readily available. Some people eschew the ties of the law altogether.

These are the facts considered in this book, which is based on a series of articles which appeared in *The Guardian* in 1968. Various important writers approach the subject from different complementary positions. Perhaps even more striking are some anonymous contributions from readers of *The Guardian,* which are outstanding in the immediacy of their deeply personal narrative.

The series included a questionnaire, and the book closes with an analysis of the responses, the results of which included some surprises.

CONTENTS

Comments on the Marriage Menders
"Freud I Call the Higher Common Sense"
Evelyn Home Talks to Ann Shearer
Forsaking All Other
We Stayed Married
Right to the Brink and Back
The Cereal Packet Norm
Our Marriage Survived Adultery
The Marriage Market
What About the Children?
What Children Have to Say About Divorce
Two Generations of Disaster
The Home I May Break Up
Divorce on the Proverty Line
After the Proceedings are Over

MARRIAGE AND DIVORCE, by Hugh Carter and Paul C. Glick. (A social-economic study Vital & Health Statistics Monographs, American Public Health Assn.)

HARVARD UNIVERSITY PRESS
79 GARDEN STREET
CAMBRIDGE, MASS. 02138
1970, $8.50 145 pp.

Marriage and divorce reporting for the United States has been complicated by the fact that each of the states has its own laws and its own enforcement and reporting procedures. Authors Carter and Glick provide in this volume the most comprehensive and systematic coverage available of up-to-date information on the demographic—social and economic—aspects of marriage, divorce, and widowhood. Focusing on behavior during marriage and the young adult through middle years of life, when most first marriages, divorces, and remarriages occur, the study explores the relative importance of various demographic elements in promoting marriage at mature adult ages and in explaining circumstances where marriages tend to fail.

Comparisons of the strengths and weaknesses of Negro and white marriage behavior are featured throughout most of the book. A chapter on persons who never marry has been included along with a chapter containing previously unpublished tables on relationships between marital status and health, with interpretive comment on social and psychological factors which are reflected through these relationships.

Many significant but little known facts about marriage are brought out in this work, for instance: being rich does not seem to make marriage stable so much as being poor makes marriage unstable; bachelors and spinsters are becoming fewer and fewer; dropping out of high school or college increases the chance for a disrupted marriage. The authors have not attempted to exhaust the possibilities for analysis of the rich sources drawn upon from census and vital records. Rather they present carefully selected illustrative material which they feel will encourage readers to return to the original sources for further study.

Sociologists, psychologists, marriage counselors, and practitioners in the medical and health fields, as well as demographers, will find this study invaluable, as will undergraduate and graduate students in the related areas.

Hugh Carter was formerly Chief of the Marriage and Divorce Statistics Branch, U.S. Public Health Service. He has taught sociology at the University of Pennsylvania, Haverford College, American University, and Purdue University and is currently self-employed as a writer and researcher in Washington, D.C.

Paul C. Glick is Assistant Chief for Demographic and Social Statistics Programs with the U.S. Bureau of the Census and has a Civil Service Commission classification as Statistician in Demography.

MARRIAGE AND DIVORCE REGISTRATION IN THE U.S., U.S. National Center for Health Statistics

U.S. DEPT. OF HEALTH, EDUCATION, AND WELFARE
PUBLIC HEALTH SERVICE
330 INDEPENDENCE AVE. S.W.
WASHINGTON, D. C.
23 pp.

Marriage and divorce are legal acts marking the beginning and termination of the family relationship, which forms the basis for the social and economic institutions of the United States. If we are to gain a more comprehensive understanding of our society, we must better understand the family, its formation through marriage and its dissolution by divorce. We must study the associated problems: the effects of hasty marriages and divorces, the effects of divorce on children, the effects of marriage and divorce on physical and mental health, and the effects of marriage and divorce on the economic and social structure of the population.

CONTENTS

1. What Do We Know About Marriage and Divorce in the United States.
2. How Marriage and Divorce Information Is Obtained.
3. Divorce Registration Area: 1965
4. Marriage and Divorce Rates in the United States: 1920–62.
5. Highlights of Marriage and Divorce Registration in the United States.
6. Establishment of Central Files in Registration Areas.

Complete reporting of marriages and divorces from all registration areas of the United States will give us greater understanding of several important social problems.

By studying the factors affecting marriage and divorce, we will be better able to plan for future population changes, develop public health programs, and understand family formation and dissolution, as they affect the individual, the family, the community, the State and the Nation.

MARRIAGE AND DIVORCE STATISTICS AND THE HEALTH DEPARTMENT, by Alice M. Hetzel

THE U.S. DEPARTMENT OF HEALTH, EDUCATION AND WELFARE
PUBLIC HEALTH SERVICE
HEALTH SERVICES AND MENTAL HEALTH ADMINISTRATION
ROCKVILLE, MARYLAND
1971

In its recent reports, "Needs for National Studies of Population Dynamics," the U.S. National Committee on Vital and Health Statistics stated: (1) "The family performs many functions that are directly revelant to population dynamics. It is the primary institution into which children are born and prepared for adult life. It is the only social grouping that man usually takes with him when he moves. Because of the importance of this basic institution in shaping the growth and distribution of our population, statistics on family formation and dissolution are essential to an adequate understanding of the nature, determinants, and the consequences of population dynamics. However, data now available are not sufficient to measure trends on differentials in various phenomena associated with the family. . . ."

This statement reflects acute awareness of the direct and profound effect of family-unit formation and dissolution on population trends. It indicates intensified interest of demographers in the socioeconomic characteristics of person who contract and dissolve marriage.

CONTENTS

Miss Hetzel *is Chief, Marriage and Divorce Statistics Branch, Division of Vital Statistics, National Center for Health Statistics, Health Services and Mental Health Administration, Public Health Service. Tearsheet requests to Miss Alice Hetzel, 5600 Fisher Lane, Rockville, Md. 20852.*

MARRIAGE COUNSELING AND CONCILIATION

(Known court-connected services with summaries of statutes and a bibliography), by Rhonda Goodkin Lorinczi

AMERICAN BAR FOUNDATION
AMERICAN BAR CENTER
1155 EAST 60TH ST.
CHICAGO, ILL. 60621
1970, 50 cents

On the basis of information collected during the course of this study, there are 154 marriage counseling services which have a formal connection to courts exercising divorce jurisdiction. This total figure includes the 72 counties in Wisconsin in which Family Court Commissioners bear a responsibility to attempt a reconciliation in each instance where an action for divorce is commenced, as well as a number of services whose exact character is unknown to us. The 154 services exist in 24 states and the Commonwealth of Puerto Rico. When the services attached to courts which do not exercise divorce jurisdiction are included, the total number of known services is increased to 159 in 28 states.

The bibliography was prepared as a part of the American Bar Foundation's study of court-connected marriage counseling in the United States. Therefore, the major criterion for selection was relevance to the purposes of that study. Very little has been published which deals directly with court-connected counseling, so most of the material is intended to provide a frame of reference for the study.

SECTIONS OF THE BIBLIOGRAPHY

Marriage and Marital Problems
Marital Adjustment and Maladjustment
Marriage Counseling and Therapy
Marriage Counseling Services
Marriage Counseling Methods
The Legal Profession and Divorce and Marriage Counseling
Divorce Law and Divorce Reform
Court-Connected Marriage Counseling

(Editor's note: *The above bibliography provides information on articles pertaining to divorce that have been published in magazines and other periodical literature.)*

MARRIAGE COUNSELING: NEW DIMENSIONS IN THE ART OF HELPING PEOPLE, by Donald L. Taylor, Phd.

CHARLES C. THOMAS
301–327 EAST LAWRENCE AVE.
SPRINGFIELD, ILL. 62703
1965, $6.75

"Marriage Counseling" offers *practical direction* to a variety of professional personnel . . . to doctors, ministers, educators, psychologists, sociologists, social workers, lawyers. It brings to the art of counseling the dimension of reciprocity—*the consideration of two people taken together.* The explanation of how reciprocity can be used in counseling is a unique feature of the book. Cultural and social dimensions are considered in detail. The author *SHOWS HOW* TO ESTABLISH AN EFFECTIVE CLIENT-COUNSELOR RELATIONSHIP. He discusses *communication,* the *problems of feeling,* and *personality* as they affect the marriage relationship. In the final chapter he sets forth a philosophy of marriage . . . contrasting the value of emphasizing ego decisions with the traditional value of agreement between husband and wife.

CONTENTS

Donald L. Taylor, Ph.D. *is Professor, Behavioral Sciences Faculty, Edwardsville Campus, Southern Illinois University, Edwardsville, Illinois.*

MARRIAGE IS THE FIRST STEP TO DIVORCE, by Pamela Mason

PAUL S. ERIKSSON, INC.
119 W. 57TH STREET
NEW YORK, N.Y. 10019
1968, $5.00
AVON BOOKS
75 cents in paperback 194 pp.

This an indefensible book. It says everything that people don't want to know about themselves or their mates or their marriage—for better "or worse" which, delightfully iconoclastic Pamela Mason insists, it almost always is.

"With a man, it's a question of 'Who's going to be there to warm my dinner?' and 'Who's going to cuddle me when my toes are cold at night?' and 'Who's going to pander my pride, see that my shirts are clean and love me no matter how stupid and egotistical I show myself to be?' "

This is a venomous book, strictly from raw scorn for males in general and husbands in particular. It tears the masculine ego to shreds; it lambastes the husband's role in American life; it derides the idea that love and marriage have anything to do with each other, or love and sex, or even sex and marriage.

"I know very little about women except what I've heard. But, in my opinion, there has never been a frigid woman in the world."

Pamela Mason leaves very little unsaid about married life that has been unsaid before. Does her book have an affirmative, positive-thinking, faith for tomorrow? No.

"Most women, when looking at other people's husbands showing off think 'Oh why couldn't I have a husband like that?' Well, the only thing I'm quite sure of is that if you did, you'd find he wasn't like that at home."

If you're looking for warmth and sweetness and orange blossoms, forget this panegyric. But if you want a first-hand glimpse of the brutal truth—as one charming ex-wife has found it to be in the hard light of the morning after, this is for you.

CONTENTS

3. Marriage is Bedlam
4. Marriage is a Delicate Condition
5. Marriage is for Bosom Pals
6. Marriage is a State of Hate
7. Marriage is a Secret Sorrow
8. Marriage is a Push Button Affair
9. Marriage is Not a Freeway
10. Marriage is a Deep Freeze
11. Marriage is an Old Fashioned Custom
12. Marriage is for Make Believe
13. Marriage is a Scavenger Hunt
14. Marriage is Not Advisable
15. Marriage is the First Step Toward Divorce
16. Marriage is an Impermanent Wave

MOTHERS ON THEIR OWN, Elbrun Rochford

HARPER & ROW, 1953
out of print at this time

This book will be a Godsend to the countless widowed and divorced mothers who suddenly find themselves left on their own resources. Writing from her own trial-and-error experience, Elbrun Rochford anticipates the myriad emergencies and decisions —financial, domestic, and personal—that confront a mother who must be breadwinner, housekeeper, and nurse all at once.

Frank and detailed in her approach to every problem, the author guides the reader through each step in getting the home and family re-established. She tells where and how to get cash for the immediate problems of housing, food, and clothing. She describes numerous living arrangements that offer healthy environments for the children and still fall within the family budget. Mothers beset with the necessity of earning a living at home will find here a variety of practical money-making ideas that have set many women up in business.

A frank discussion of how to cope with the problems of fatherless children will be invaluable to mothers concerned about the emotional health and balanced outlook of their children. Finally, the book offers helpful advice on how to take advantage of community services for children and how to plan intelligently for a child's education, and presents sound counsel on the legal problems of women in general, with particular reference to the mother on her own.

CONTENTS

1. The First Few Steps
2. Establishing Your Home
3. Mother as the Breadwinner
4. Life with Your Children
5. Your Fatherless Children's Problems
6. Short Cuts to Good Living
7. Civic and Community Advantages for Your Child
8. Education
9. Your Legal Problems

THE MUSLIM MATRIMONIAL COURT IN SINGAPORE,
by Judith Djamour

HUMANITIES PRESS
303 PARK AVENUE SOUTH
NEW YORK, NEW YORK 10010
1966, $6.25

This book is an anthropologist's field study of the new court set up in Singapore to deal with matrimonial suits (chiefly divorce) among Muslims. The study is based on careful observation of the court in action, and analyses in detail the relationship between the reformist aims of the new law and the values and expectations of litigants. The book takes its departure from the argument developed in Dr. Djamour's earlier work, "Malay Kinship and Marriage in Singapore" (Atholne Press, 1959; paper back edition 1965), and discusses the effect of recent attempts to promote the stability of Muslim marriage. Social scientists, lawyers, students of Islam, and those interested in Malayan problems will find in this book the same qualities that distinguished Dr. Djamour's previous study—lively and sympathetic description powers joined to an ability for clear, factual analysis.

CONTENTS

THE OLD LOVE AND THE NEW: DIVORCE AND READJUSTMENT, by Willard Waller

SOUTHERN ILLINOIS UNIVERSITY PRESS
CARBONDALE, ILL. 62901
1967, $7.00 331 pp.

An original and valuable work when first published in 1930, "The Old Love and the New" throughout a quarter of a century constituted the entire body of sociological research on personal adjustment after divorce and remains today a major work in that field. Bernard Farber, who has himself made significant contributions to the sociology of the family, ably introduces this new edition and relates Waller's effect on subsequent research.

In this study, Willard Waller shifted the focus from divorce as a social problem, as it had been discussed previously, to divorce as an event in an individual's life history, and thus broke ground in providing for the general reader an understanding of the problems encountered after disorganization of a marriage. "It is a good book and a brave book, rich in the kind of material which is creating a new understanding of human nature," said one critic.

Waller perceives divorce as analogous to surgery. Although the individual who has had an operation would have been better off had he not needed one, he has no choice but to recuperate. In accordance with this view, Waller is concerned with the means of adjustment. He discusses the effective utilization of the experience of divorce and the minimizing of personal and social costs. For the author, divorce implies change—and change, in turn, implies crisis, disorganization, and reorganization. He explains divorce—the legal break—as only one point in a long process which begins with alienation from one's spouse and lasts until readjustment is complete. Basing his analysis on case histories and a sparing use of dynamic psychiatry, he describes what happens socially and psychologically to the divorced man or woman in the attempts to readjust: the shifting of friendships, sexual adjustment, economic problems, search for a proper role in society, transfer of affections, and in some cases, remarriage.

Because today the problems encountered by the divorced person are similar to those of a generation ago, Waller's observations remain sound. The divorcee, in particular, quickly discovers she must tread a rough path in a complex social world. She is called upon to fulfill an awesome array of roles—and always under the gaze of a society that often lacks sympathy.

Willard Waller was ahead of his time and anticipated some of the major developments in family sociology which are current today. Many of his insights are relevant to other kinds of family problems as well as divorce. His work has remained the basis of subsequent research, and republication of this volume will thus provide a solid background for contemporary sociologists. In his introduction Bernard Farber discusses both earlier and later studies, writing a succinct essay on this entire field which will contribute to the understanding of both the sociologist and the general reader.

CONTENTS

Bernard Farber, *who received his Ph.D. from the University of Chicago, is Professor of Sociology and a member of the Institute for Research on Exceptional Children at the University of Illinois. His research has focused on effects of mentally retarded children on family relationships, and he is the author of "Family: Organization and Interaction" and editor of "Kinship and Family Organization." Professor Farber has also contributed to the sociological literature on research technique, ecology, social class and intelligence, and kinship. Herman R. Lantz is the General Editor of this "Perspectives in Sociology" series. He is professor of Sociology at Southern Illinois University.*

THE ONE-PARENT FAMILY, by Benjamin Schlesinger

UNIVERSITY OF TORONTO PRESS
UNIVERSITY OF TORONTO
TORONTO, 181, ONTARIO, CANADA
1970, $6.00 132 pp.

About 13 per cent of American families and 9 per cent of Canadian families can be classified as one-parent families through desertion, separation, death, divorce, or an unmarried mother situation. Until the publication of this bibliography there has been a dearth of collected information on the subject.

From 1965 to 1968 Dr. Schlesinger was consultant to two groups of social work students who completed the first Canadian studies on one-parent families and on remarriage. It was at this time that he realized the problems which one-parent families had to face and also the need for systematic information in these fields.

His book includes a general essay by himself on the one-parent family in North America, one by Jetse Sprey on methods of research in this field, and a third paper by Felix M. Berardo on widowhood status in North America. In this edition, an addendum to the annotated bibliography is included, and a brief description of the new divorce law in Canada has been added as Appendix VIII. The bibliography section includes 314 annotations of books, pamphlets, journal articles, and statistical data on one-parent families, remarriage, and Parents Without Partners, an international organization of single parents.

Social agencies, child guidance clinics, and social planning councils will find this an invaluable reference tool.

CONTENTS

Benjamin Schlesinger *received his B.A. in 1951 from Sir George Williams College and his Master of Social Work degree from the University of Toronto in 1953. After three years with the Children's Aid Society in Toronto he did a year's postgraduate study as an intern in psychotherapy and marriage counseling at the Merrill-Palmer Institute in Detroit. He was awarded his doctorate from Cornell in 1961 in child development and family relationships. He is at present Professor of Social Work and Chairman of the teaching area of Human Behaviour and Social Environment at the University of Toronto.*

For divorced, separated, and widowed parents, the crucial questions are these:

- What makes a workable separation agreement?
- How can some of the financial problems of single parenthood be solved?
- Why are single parents (and their children!) apt to feel different?
- Where may single parents turn for help or guidance on the many problems involved in divorce, separation, widowhood?
- How can divorced fathers remain parents to their children?
- How can widowed parents help their children accept the loss of a parent?
- What do children of single parents think about their mothers and fathers?
- How can the divided or one-parent family still be a family?
- Why do children of divorce need their fathers?
- How can remarriage be more a solution and less a complication to the problems of single parenthood?

This book, for the first time, presents the combined viewpoint of both fathers and mothers in a sound and sensible discussion of possible answers to the single parent problems. To find them, the authors have drawn on personal experiences of single parents as well as information plus insight gained through association with a unique organization—Parents Without Partners, Inc.

PWP was started four and a half years ago by a small group of single parents who came together to discuss the special problems of divided and one-parent families. From this nucleus developed a national organization of almost 40 chapters with total membership now in the thousands. It provided, for the first time, a forum where divorced, widowed and separated mothers and fathers could exchange ideas and experiences not only among themselves but also with specialists in medicine, law, child behavior and human relations, *Jim Egleson* co-founder and first president of the organization, helped to establish a program of genuine benefit to all single parents and their children. *Janet Frank Egleson*, who became a member during the first year, helped to publicize this program and to edit and expand the 'PWP Journal'.

From their combined experience, the authors have fashioned a practical, helpful, and constructive guide. Special features include a model separation agreement drafted by attorney Charles Rothenberg, specialist in marital and divorce law; a chapter on "The PWP Idea"; a chapter on "Getting Together with Other Single Parents". The Eglesons have also consulted widely with experts in child development and human behavior and have used generous amounts of case-history material obtained from parents who are or have been divorced, separated, or widowed. The result is a book that will not only help single parents and their children to understand and solve their problems, but will also interest relatives, friends, and the community at large—in which the divided or one-parent family can and should play an integral part.

CONTENTS

POSITIVE DIVORCE REFORM FOR AMERICA, by Lester C. Kohut

ASSOCIATION FOR THE ADVANCEMENT OF FAMILY STABILITY
FAMILY LAW PUBLICATIONS
P.O. BOX 2192, MADISON, WISC. 53701
1969, $1.00

Legislatures, professional associations and various other groups of people across the land are taking a serious look at their divorce problems and their divorce laws and practices. The Illinois Legislature and former Governor Otto Kerner are to be commended for creating this Family Study Commission on Marriage, Divorce, and Parental Responsibility.

As Mr. Kohut remarks, "We think we should emphasize at the outset that this brief represents an interdisciplinary approach to divorce, and hence what we say may either be above your heads or it may be unpalatable. We sincerely hope, in spite of the composition of the membership of this Commission, that you will have an open mind to our proposals. We are here in the cause of family stability and not with any particular axe to grind or vested interested to protect. Several years of thinking and several months of solid work went into this brief and we hope that it gets the attention it deserves. We would like to emphasize that creative and hard research went into this report."

CONTENTS

1. Abolish grounds for divorce and substitute a general breakdown as the basis for divorce
2. Society must devise new divorce tribunals

V. JUSTIFICATION FOR DIVORCE TRIBUNALS
1. Several persons needed to determine breakdown competently
2. Tribunal duty as civic responsibility
3. Social welfare comes before private welfare
4. Society must exhaust every reasonable effort

VI. SOME PROTOTYPES

VII. SOME OBJECTIONS TO DIVORCE TRIBUNALS

VIII. CONCLUSIONS AND RECOMMENDATIONS
Establish Illinois Council for Home and Family

APPENDIX A—Letter-head of Wisconsin Council for Home and Family and press cut-out on Wisconsin's Family Code Study Committee of 1957.

APPENDIX B—Copy of enabling legislation creating the Wisconsin Council for Home and Family.

For the author's background see "A Manual on Marital Reconciliations."

A PROGRAMMED GUIDE TO DIVORCE, by Anonymous

SPHERE BOOKS, LTD., 1970
out of print at this time

It is an old saying that in marriage there is one who loves and one who is loved, but it is just as true to say that there is one who married and one who was (and is) married—and doesn't really want to be. Many of these people accept marriage because they are in love and fell for that first wave of enthusiasm—suckers for the hard sell of passion and desire. But just as many give in to what we might call a soft sell and marry from a sense of pity (they can't bear to hurt by saying no) or duty (everyone else seems to expect it) or resignation (they can't fight any more) or despair (what else is there?).

The enthusiastic ones, bowled over by what turned out to be a short lived passion, have spectacular fights and reconciliations. Life for them is unpredictable and (they say) exciting. Nothing is so sweet as the kiss that forgives, etc.—though really it falls logically into the hair-of-the-dog class of pleasure, in which the first drink tastes ambrosial against the acrid and masochistic sensation of a throbbing hangover. But even they may settle down in time.

The suckers for the soft sell often have the most stable marriages of all. They knew what kind of contract they were signing. But now and again one of these suckers wakes up one day with a clear light of recognition in his eye. He wants out, particularly if in the meantime he has realised what he should have done in the first place. Does this sound familiar? Do you recognise yourself? Read on.

Unfortunately society is emotional and not responsible, and although divorces for purely negative reasons like cruelty, incompatibility, or adultery are allowed and in some sectors even encouraged, divorce for positive and logical reasons is seen as cruel and impossible. Indeed, if a hen-pecked husband, who has for years supported a stable marriage by forebearance and generosity, quietly walks out to a new life and better life, everyone's sympathy and society's official support goes to the harridan he left behind.

So you need to arrange matters so that you can leave without seeming to be the ogre that you are not—and also without paying alimony to an unjustified and crippling extent (how many marriages are preserved by the amount of alimony that the departing husband would not be able to afford?). This book tries to show, step by step, how to get free from an apparently impossible situation in the shortest possible time compatible with seeming-to-be in the right. Like all self instructional books, it should not be read from page to page, but should be followed through according to the instructions. At the end of this lesson on the first page there is a question. Choose the answer you think is right. You will then be told which page to look at.

CONTENTS

THE PSYCHOTHERAPIES OF MARITAL DISHARMONY, edited by Bernard L. Greene, MD

MACMILLAN
866 THIRD AVENUE
NEW YORK, N.Y. 10022
1965, $7.95 191 pp.

Never before has the work of so many leading psychoanalysts, psychiatrists, sociologists, and social workers, all writing on the treatment of marital problems, been gathered under one cover. These writers' contributions constitute a unique presentation of the various therapeutic methods employed in dealing with marital disharmony.

The very diversity of contributors is this volume's most notable feature, for it is the tremendous variation in marital patterns, the differences among individual couples, that necessitates greater flexibility in technique to cope best with each situation.

Thus, the collection first considers supportive therapy—counseling that stresses sociocultural forces. Intensive therapy is then examined: classic psychoanalysis, the individual-oriented approach. The contributors also consider collaborative therapy, in which each marriage partner is treated by different therapists who communicate with each other; concurrent therapy in which partners are seen together; combined therapy, which includes individual, concurrent, and conjoint sessions; and analytic family therapy.

CONTENTS

6. Concurrent Psychoanalytic Therapy in Marital Disharmony—Alfred P. Solomon and Bernard L. Greene
7. Conjoint Marital Therapy—Virginia M. Satir
8. Treatment of Marital Disharmony: The Use of Individual, Concurrent, and Conjoint Sessions as a "Combined Approach"—Bernard L. Greene, Betty P. Broadhurst, and Noel Lustig
9. The Family Approach to Marital Disorders—Nathan W. Ackerman
10. Clinical Illustrations from Psychoanalytic Family Therapy—Martin Grotjahn

Bernard L. Greene, M.D., *the editor of this volume and one of the contributors, is Assistant Clinical Professor of Psychiatry at the College of Medicine, University of Illinois. He is also Chief of the Marital Department, Forest Hospital, Des Plaines, Illinois.*

RAISING YOUR CHILD IN A FATHERLESS HOME, by Eve Jones

THE FREE PRESS OF GLENCOE
A DIVISION OF THE MACMILLAN COMPANY.
866 THIRD AVE.
NEW YORK, N.Y. 10022
1963, $4.95

Here is a clear and complete discussion of the daily life of the single woman—divorced, separated, widowed, or unmarried—and the problems she faces in raising her child in a fatherless home.

Dr. Jones offers a reassuring guide to the solution of emotional difficulties caused by the single mother's reactions to the particular pressures of her life. She stresses the importance of examining overall expectations and treats in careful detail the aids a single mother may use to achieve emotional well-being and health for herself and her child. Professional consultation is only one of the many aids Dr. Jones describes.

After tracing the usual physical and psychological development of a child within the ordinary complete family, she explains the variations on this pattern that inevitably arise in the fatherless home.

This book will prove a valuable guide—and welcome solace—to any woman facing the burden of lonely parenthood.

CONTENTS

Eve Jones *is well known for her nationally syndicated daily newspaper column, 'Parents' World,' and for her television and radio series. She obtained her Ph.D. in clinical psychology from the University of Chicago where she also studied medicine. She has been a member of the faculty for more than eight years, devoting her primary attention to the psychoanalytic personality theories.*

Her experience as a mother of four children, as a participant in numerous research projects, and as a consultant in psychodiagnostics for emotionally disturbed children at the Sonia Shankman Orthogenic School, under the direction of Dr. Bruno Bettelheim, has provided her with a broad understanding of both normal and abnormal parent-child relationships. Dr. Jones is the author of "The Intelligent Parents' Guide to Raising Children." In private life, she is Mrs. William D. Bonner.

THE ROAD TO RENO, by Nelson Manfred Blake (A history of Divorce in the U.S.)

THE MACMILLAN COMPANY, 1962.
out of print at this time.

Why is it so easy to obtain a divorce in Nevada and so difficult to get one—honestly—in New York State? Why have all the attempts to establish a uniform national divorce law failed? It is to these questions and their answers that this book addresses itself.

Divorce is as old as marriage. Roman law, Jewish tradition, medieval Christian dogma, and Protestant polemies all contributed to widely divergent attitudes. In this highly informative study, the author shows how these conflicting ideas were carried to the American colonies and how they resulted in local differences, ranging from Puritan New England, where divorce was sometimes permitted, to the Anglican South, where no provision for the termination of an unhappy marriage was made at all.

After the Revolutionary War, most states provided for the dissolution of marriages either through special acts of the state legislature or through the regular courts. South Carolina's no-divorce policy and New York's one-ground divorce law were unique. This book deals extensively with the New York situation, describing numerous unsuccessful attempts to liberalize the law. The author shows how New York conservatism has resulted in widespread perjury and an increasing migration of the unhappily married to the courts of other states.

Mr. Blake describes the long and colorful history of migratory divorce. He explores the reasons why certain states such as Illinois, Indiana, South Dakota, and notorious Nevada allow quickie-divorce decrees. He also explains the reasons why the Supreme Court's attempts to solve these problems have only added to the confusion.

The Road to Reno takes a hard look at the American divorce question and provides some realistic suggestions for putting divorce on a more humane and rational basis.

CONTENTS

Nelson Blake *is a Professor of History at Syracuse University. He has written many books on American life, among them, Since 1900:* A history of the United States in Our Times, *with Oscar T. Barck as co-author. He is well known for his many articles in American historical journals and periodicals.*

From the book, SINGLE AGAIN, by Howard Lyman

DAVID MCKAY COMPANY, INC.
850 THIRD AVENUE
NEW YORK, N.Y. 10017
1971, $6.95

"Single Again" is for those who need the insight and practical advice of someone who knows the ins and outs of going it alone. Howard Lyman, a psychologist who has been through a divorce and lived to tell about it, has written a compassionate, wise, and always optimistic book based on his own experiences and those of others similarly situated in life—namely, the divorced or widowed.

Dr. Lyman offers a basic crash course in self-preservation, telling the single-againer how to avoid cherishing hurt, how to overcome shock, self-pity, wounded pride, guilt, distrust, and withdrawal.

There is a wealth of advice for the woman alone, often more vulnerable than the man: how to overcome the "fifth-wheel" or "left-out" feeling in groups, form new relationships with old friends, cope with patronizing attitudes in others, keep from imposing on married friends, deal with the distrust of married women, keep from being exploited sexually or socially.

For a man alone there is similar counsel on how to adjust to the change, seek a new social life, consider remarriage, and achieve emotional independence. For both men and women there is detailed advice on handling children on your own, particularly if you are a parent who works.

"Single Again" describes the complete preparatory steps a couple must take when contemplating divorce: what to tell the children and how to choose a good lawyer and arrange your financial situation.

For the single-againer, there are always questions about sex. Dr. Lyman answers them honestly, including how to get back into the dating game and how to evaluate single-again groups all over the country.

CONTENTS

Dr. Howard B. Lyman, *who teaches in the Department of Psychology at the University of Cincinnati and is a past president of the Ohio and Cincinnati Psychological Associations, has published previous books, many articles, and edited journals in the fields of psychology and educational testing. He is active in several guidance organizations.*

THE SINGLE WOMAN: HER ADJUSTMENT TO LIFE AND LOVE, by Dr. Laura Hutton

ROY PUBLISHERS, INC.
30 EAST 74TH STREET
NEW YORK, N.Y. 10021
1962, $3.50

Loneliness and how to adjust, emotionally, sexually, socially—these are the problems of the single woman in her forties and older. While countless books have been written on the problems of married couples, the equally troubling problems of the single woman remain strangely neglected. In Dr. Hutton's frank and enlightening book, single women will find facts and points of view which can hardly fail to be of particular value to them.

Unmarried women who work for their living are a product of modern civilization. As teachers, doctors, social workers, in administrative positions, business or responsible secretarial work, thousands of self-supporting women of mature age make important contributions to the life of their communities. To these women the prospect of marriage, although not necessarily extinct, is not to be counted on. They must be prepared to live out their lives as best they can, without the natural adequate fulfillment of their normal physiological functions as women.

Dr. Hutton's outspoken views on how to cope with these problems are bound to be controversial. At the very least, her book will help establish a platform where all aspects of the situation can be discussed openly and without prejudice. And for many a lonely single woman who believes that happiness is beyond her reach, this book will bring the release and peace of mind that comes with self-understanding.

CONTENTS

Sex in Women's Friendships
The Physical Aspect
The Emotional Aspect
The Moral Aspect
The Social Aspect

SEXUAL INVERSION

Theories of the Origin of Sexual Inversion
Sexual Inversion, Perversion, and Neurosis
Psychogenic Factors in Homosexuality
Types of Homosexual Women
Homosexuality, Alcoholism, and Drug Addiction

STATISTICAL ANALYSIS OF AMERICAN DIVORCE, by Alfred Cahen

ORIGINALLY PUBLISHED BY COLUMBIA UNIVERSITY PRESS, 1932
A M S PRESS
56 EAST 13TH STREET
NEW YORK, N.Y. 10003
1968, 146 pp.

This dissertation is the only current statistical survey of the United States Census divorce records from the Civil War to the present time. The approach to this problem in social causation is primarily quantitative, although many viewpoints are examined. This population study is concerned with the adjustment of the institution of the family to changing environmental conditions. Finally, the purpose of this monograph is to analyze the statistics and interpret the facts of our modern American divorce phenomena.

CONTENTS

THERAPEUTIC FAMILY LAW—A COMPLETE GUIDE TO MARITAL RECONCILIATIONS, edited by Lester C. Kohut

FAMILY LAW PUBLICATIONS
P.O. BOX 2192
MADISON, WISC. 53701
1968, $9.95 436 pp.

Note these points about our divorce scene:

1. Divorce is an epidemic
2. Our ever-legalistic approach is essentially negative and non-helpful
3. Many people seeking a divorce are seeking help—not a divorce
4. Many professionals, especially the clergy, are excluded from helping in divorce work
5. Non-fault divorce is being bandied around a good bit today, but few know its deeper ramifications.

Therapeutic Family Law is aimed to inform you on two basic issues tied up with the five above observations:

1. The TEAM approach to divorce—especially how and when to refer and how you can assist the attorney with divorce cases
2. NON-FAULT divorce—especially viability and revivability of marriage and tests of breakdown (first comprehensive discussion)

CONTENTS

11. Some fundamentals of counseling
12. Some techniques of counseling
13. Critical phases in marriage counseling—Robert G. Foster, Ph.D.
14. Strategy and perception in divorce cases—Robert Redmount, Ph.D.
15. How the psychologist can assist the attorney in divorce cases—Nathan Hurvitz, Ph.D.
16. How the social worker can assist the attorney in divorce cases—Meyer Elkin, M.S.W.
17. How the psychiatrist can assist the attorney in divorce cases—Rudolph Dreikurs, M.D.
18. The role of the trial judge in reconciling parties headed for divorce—Justice Robert W. Hansen, Wisconsin Supreme Court
19. How the physician can assist the attorney in rehabilitating broken marriages—Marianne S. Breslin, M.D.
20. How the pastoral counselor can assist the attorney in rehabilitating broken marriages—A Catholic view—Msgr. Cliff Sawher, MA
21. How the pastoral counselor can assist the attorney in rehabilitating broken marriages—a Protestant view—R. Lofton Hudson, Ph.D.
22. How the pastoral counselor can assist the attorney in rehabilitating broken marriages—a Jewish view—Rabbi Harry Essrig, Ph.D.
23. The attorney and alcoholic marriages—John A. Ewing M.D.
24. Children's welfare—Kenneth D. Johnson
25. Children and divorce—Philip Polatin, M.D. & Ellen Philtine, M.D.
26. Toward a marriage breakdown inventory—Nathan W. Ackerman, M.D.
27. The therapeutic separation agreement
28. The reconciliation agreement—Justice Louis H. Burke
29. A case of administrative family law—Mary Sitton and Tom Martinez
30. Divorce for the broken marriage
31. Some additional constructive proposals
32. How the attorney can represent the husband in divorce cases—Charles V. Metz
33. Epilogue
34. Cases on the other woman—American Association of Marriage Counselors
35. Case on an immature couple—American Association of Marriage Counselors

WHEN PARENTS DIVORCE: A NEW APPROACH TO NEW RELATIONSHIPS, by Bernard Steinzor

PANTHEON BOOKS
201 EAST 50TH ST.
NEW YORK, N.Y. 10022
1969, $5.95 $1.25 paperback 243 pp.

The radically new views outlined in this compassionate handbook relate intimately to the lives of thousands of divorced parents now engaged in desperate efforts to continue the doomed relationship with former partners "for the sake of the children." Dr. Steinzor, a psychologist and family counselor, rejects the well-meaning but harmful advice of a multitude of therapists when he firmly insists that both parents and children should face reality without pretense; divorce based on artificial friendship with the former partner, he argues, is no solution. This penetrating examination of the total marriage relationship sets the stage for a revolution that would bring attitudes about divorce into line with the actualities of American life today. "When Parents Divorce" also includes practical selections on choosing a lawyer, writing the separation agreement, providing for child support, living independently after divorce, and remarrying. A refreshingly honest, helpful book.

CONTENTS

Bernard Steinzor *was born in 1920. He was graduated Phi Beta Kappa from the College of the City of New York and received his doctorate from the University of Chicago. He has taught at Sarah Lawrence and the Univer-*

sity of Chicago and was a lecturer at the Menninger Clinic and a staff member of the U. S. Air Force Psychological Research-Unit. A member of the New York State Board of Examiners of Psychologists, Dr. Steinzor lectures both at Columbia University Department of Psychiatry and at Union Theological Seminary and maintains a full-time practice in psychotherapy. His first book, "The Healing Partnership: Psychotherapy and the Value of Equality," was published in 1967. His articles have appeared in anthologies and numerous professional journals. Dr. Steinzor is married and has three children.

WHERE IS DADDY?, by Beth Goff (juvenile literature)

BEACON PRESS
25 BEACON STREET
BOSTON, MASS. 02108
1969, $3.95

Once there was a little girl called Janeydear. She lived in a house with her daddy and her mommy and a dog named Funny. But one day Daddy wasn't there any more, and Janeydear didn't understand when her Mommy told her, "You and Funny and I will be keeping house for a while." One day when her Daddy did come back, he said, "Janeydear, Mommy and I are going to get a divorce." But Janeydear didn't understand that either.

This book tells the story of what happens to Janeydear after that. It shows what happens in a family when parents get divorced. A divorce is hard to understand without getting frightened. Janeydear does get frightened and confused, but she learns at last to understand a little better and be happy again.

"Where is Daddy" is a unique read-aloud for children of divorcing parents which can help a child understand and accept the events and changes that initially appear as insurmountable obstacles and powerful threats to his security.

Beth Goff, *a psychiatric social worker in child guidance, wrote this story to help a child who had become severely withdrawn and unreachable following her parents' divorce; Mrs. Goff's success with the story encouraged her to use it with other children of divorcing parents. But "Where is Daddy?" is more than a helpful approach to a child's psychological crisis; it is a touching story, augmented by Susan Perl's sensitive drawings, which will win the sympathy and affection of children and adults alike.*

In an afterword for parents, John F. McDermott, Jr., M.D., Director of In-Patient Services at Childrens' Psychiatric Hospital at the University of Michigan, adds this: "Why do we feel so strongly about Janeydear? Possibly because she reflects our old childhood fear of being helpless and lonely. It is important for parents who are divorcing to recognize these fears in themselves and their child . . . The main task then, is to get parents and child back in tune with each other so that the parents understand what the child is feeling and can make their decisions on this basis. Perhaps a story such as this can serve as a bridge, helping parents and child to put back in perspective what has become distorted."

WHY DIVORCE OR SEPARATION?, by Henry Traskos

CARLTON PRESS
84 FIFTH AVE.
NEW YORK, N.Y. 10010
1969, $2.00 54 pp.

Many years ago someone defined marriage as "that relation between man and woman in which the independence is equal, the dependence mutual, and the obligation reciprocal."

That this reciprocity—or the lack of it—often determines the failure or success of this oldest and most important of man's institutions is the theme of Henry Traskos' logical and candid book, Why Divorce or Separation?

"Marriage is a wonderful thing, so take good care of each other," is the kernel of wisdom of Mr. Traskos' advice. And in the same direct, succinct manner, he goes into related technical, social, and legal problems.

A forthright man who believes in weeding out and burying old wives' tales and superstition, he nevertheless cautions against "going overboard," pointing out that the "old-fashioned" ideas of fidelity and chastity before marriage are still the best.

However, he has not fallen victim to self-righteous sermonizing and, realizing that the abandonment of such ideas is quite widespread, he goes on to give advice on how to cope with the difficulties which threaten marriage in our complex and oftentimes confusing modern world.

Because sex is often the root of marriage problems, he devotes much time to examining marital sex—approach, techniques, and attitudes toward it—and underlines the absolute necessity of understanding the basic differences between man and woman in this matter.

A vigorously written marriage manual which avoids extremely technical terminology, "Why Divorce or Separation?" displays a workaday soundness and articulate understanding that can be successfully applied to everyday living. Hence, it should prove a welcome aid in reducing the number of divorces and separations that have broken so many homes and hearts.

CONTENTS

2. A Message for Husbands
3. Wills and Insurance
4. To Prevent Pregnancy
5. Moods of Women
6. Premenstrual Syndrome

"Why Divorce or Separation"—Henry R. Traskos' *first book—is the result of over fifteen years of listening to and advising people on the problems encountered in marriage. At one time a route salesman, the author, always concerned with the troubles of others, realized the need for a basic, common-sense marriage manual.*

Although he has lived in both California and Florida, Mr. Traskos makes his permanent home in his native Connecticut, where he was born in Middletown on August 30, 1916.

THE WOMAN ON THE VERGE OF DIVORCE, by Angela Reed

WARD LOCK LTD. IN ASSOCIATION WITH PLUME PRESS LTD. (ENGLAND)
WEST BOWERS HALL
WOODHAM WALTER, MALDON, ESSEX, ENGLAND
$9.75

So many women today are faced with problems in marriage and don't know to whom to turn for advice and help. Divorce is the ultimate way out, but is it necessary?

This book suggests answers to the many intimate questions that pose themselves during such crises. It does so with sympathy and compassion, yet in a thoroughly factual manner, because Mrs. Reed has had many years of experience of such issues.

She considers in some detail the following concerns:

What lies ahead for the woman faced with divorce?
Is there any chance at all of saving the marriage?
If not, how can she come to terms with her new situation?
The many problems which a woman regards as unique in her own case and which are, in fact, common problems.

The book aims to help and support a woman through the emotional strains and legal processes she may have to endure. It discusses the impact of divorce on her changed financial, social, and personal position and on her children, as well as the acute problem of loneliness. Detailed information is given about practical and counseling help which is available from individuals and organizations.

CONTENTS

7. The woman alone
8. Fatherless families
9. Working mothers
10. New relationships
11. Second marriage
12. Practical help

Angela Reed *has worked for the National Marriage Guidance Council for sixteen years and during that time has contributed articles on many aspects of marriage to a wide variety of magazines and journals, as well as being interviewed about the work on radio and television.*

Before that, after taking an honours degree at Oxford, she had valuable experience as a caseworker on Teesside and as an editor working on a group of magazines for the Central Office of Information. Among other things, she edits the journal "Marriage Guidance" and is working on new type publications on personal relationships for use in schools.

from WOMEN ALONE, by Isabella Taves © 1968 by Isabella Taves

FUNK & WAGNALLS PUBLISHING CO., INC.
201 PARK AVENUE SOUTH
NEW YORK, N.Y. 10003
reprinted with permission of the publisher, $5.95 316 pp.

CONTENTS

Isabella Taves, *the author of "Successful Women" and "The Quick Rich Fox" and co-author of "Three Lives of Harriet Hubbard Ayer" and "I Learned About Women from Them," has contributed articles to many national magazines. She traveled throughout America and to resorts in the Far East, South America, and Europe questioning "women alone": how they react to their new life, how they travel, where they find men, what adjustments they have made in their moral code, how they cope with their children and those of prospective husbands, where they find jobs, and how they handle money.*

The author, herself a recent widow—her husband was Dan Mich, former Senior Editor of Look*—has written a facinating book, filled with insight and sympathy.*

WOMEN IN DIVORCE, by William J. Goode

Originally published under the title "After Divorce," 1956
THE MACMILLAN COMPANY
866 THIRD AVENUE
NEW YORK, NEW YORK 10022
1965, $3.50 paperback $2.95 381 pp.

Does divorce really harm children? Does it spoil people for remarriage? What role does religion play in the life of a divorced woman? Why is the remarriage rate of divorced women so high? These are only a few of the searching questions explored in this unique and forthright work. The conclusions drawn from the author's research shatter many of our present beliefs about divorce.

"Women In Divorce" is the first major field study of what actually happens to people affected by a broken marriage. Professor Goode has conducted a thorough and objective study of divorce and its aftermath. Both the sampling techniques and the survey used in this research are included here.

Unhappily, the most rational, intelligent couple—even with the best of intentions—may not be able to make a success of their marriage. The final break may be a tragic experience. "Women in Divorce" offers a perceptive analysis of the reasons for the failure of a marriage, and, most important, of the readjustments divorced persons are forced to make.

CONTENTS

THE WORLD OF THE FORMERLY MARRIED, by
Morton M. Hunt

McGRAW-HILL
330 WEST 42ND ST.
NEW YORK, N.Y. 10036
1966, $7.95 326 pp.
75¢ paperback—FAWCETT PUBLICATIONS
1967, 256 pp.

Silence after heated words, the shutting of a suitcase, the final closing of the front door—and then what? Every married person has wondered what it would be like if differences—or—indifference tore his or her marriage apart. Where does one go, how does one feel, what does one do? What are the chances of reconciliation, of a new love, of a better life?

The answers to such questions have been largely hidden from married people because the separated and divorced are so secretive about the special world in which they live—the World of the Formerly Married. There is a reason for their discretion: they are painfully aware that their manners and morals violate many of the conventions of the larger society around them, and that their sorrows are often a bore and their joys a threat to the married.

Morton M. Hunt takes the reader on an intimate tour of this strange world, following the Formerly Married through the entire process of marital dissolution, separation, and divorce, and the various phases of their self-rediscovery and readjustment. Through the words and experiences of hundreds of actual people, he reveals surprising aspects of life in that world: the unexpected exhilaration and rejuvenation that often go hand in hand with bouts of dreadful despair; the rediscovery of passion and emotion; the therapeutic values—and potential dangers—of sexual experimentation; the special ecstasies and difficulties of love affairs among the divorced. He explores the emotional meaning of the fight over alimony and property, the potential harm—or benefit—divorce brings to children, the strength of the drive to remarry, the chances of greater success in the second marriage than in the first one.

Here is an eye-opening account of the hidden society in which one out of every four married Americans will eventually dwell. Mr. Hunt has observed and interviewed a broad range of formerly married people, reviewed the scientific findings about them, and conducted a nation-wide survey. But although research supports every statement in his book, it is written with almost novelistic intensity and immediacy; one does not merely read about the experiences of the Formerly Married here—one virtually under-goes them. "The World of the Formerly Married" shines a light in the darkness for the married, and holds the mirror up to those who are separated or divorced.

CONTENTS

YOU CAN START ALL OVER, By Marjorie Hillis Roulston

HARPER & ROW, 1951
out of print at this time

The world is full of lonely ladies—recently widowed or divorced—who have suddenly found themselves odd numbers and very forlorn indeed. This book takes up their problems with sympathy and understanding. It makes no claim that even grim determination can make everything all right over-night. But it does tell how to face a major crisis in life, and what to do about it.

If you are overwhelmed by such problems as whether to live alone, and where——
The Necessity of Finding a Job After Forty——
Mourning Conventions; or what a divorcee should do, and should not——
How to Fill Those Endless Empty Hours——
How Not to Remain a Weeping Willow for Too Long——
What to do About the Remaining Men in Your Life, If Any——
You will find answers in these pages.

Even married women may discover a few helpful hints in the brief case histories. Before you read the last page, you will be convinced that you really can start all over, and that life still can be exciting after all.

CONTENTS

Shortly before the war, Mrs. Roulston—*then Marjorie Hillis—wrote a wise, gay, and highly practical little book called "Live Alone and Like It." Hundreds of thousands of single women profited from its witty and unortho-*

dox advice. Her next book, "Orchids On Your Budget," was also a best seller.

Then she became Mrs. Roulston; and after ten years of happy married life, she suffered the loss of her husband. From her own experience, she learned all about the difficult readjustments which a great many women must face sooner or later. She has written about these problems with the wisdom, common sense, and good taste, which made her earlier books so helpful.

RECENT BOOKS

PUBLICATIONS ON DIVORCE
(Earlier U.S.)

PUBLICATIONS ON DIVORCE
(Worldwide)

Recent Books—Permission for Detailed Entry not Received as of this Printing

Baer, Jean.
Second Wives. Garden City: Doubleday, 1972.

Baguedor, Eve.
Separation: Journal of a Marriage. New York: Simon and Schuster, Inc., 1972.
219 pp.

Barrow,.
Divorce, Illegitimacy and the Child.
Wellington, New Zealand: A.H. Reed, 1968.
£0.42½

Bartlett, George Arthur.
Men, Women and Conflict. New York: G.P. Putnam's Sons, 1931.
294 pp.

Benson, Michael.
Marriage at Risk. London: P. Davies, 1958.
A book of divorce law and cases.
223 pp.

Biskind, Elliott L.
Boardman's N.Y. Family Law, with Forms. Revised Edition.
New York: C. Boardman Company, 1972.
To be kept up to date by periodic insertion of additional pages and substitution of old pages.
1500 pp. Looseleaf
$42.50

Biskind, Elliott.
The New Divorce Law. New York: C. Boardman Company, Reprint 1966.
Issued as a special supplement to his Boardman's N.Y. Family Law with Forms.
12 pp.

Boykin, James H.
Foreign Divorce. Brooklyn: Pageant Press, 1964.
74 pp.

Broel, Alexander A.-Plateris.
Divorce Statistics Analysis, United States, 1962. Washington, D.C.: U.S. Dept. of Health, Education and Welfare, 1965.
For sale by the Superintendent of Documents.
56 pp.

Bunkley, Joel William.
Amis on Divorce and Separation in Mississippi. Atlanta: Harrison Company, 1957.
505 pp.

Bureau of Vital Statistics.
Divorce in California. Berkeley: California, 1966.
186 pp. Illus.

Campbell, Litta Belle.
Whom God Hath Joined Asunder. New York: Simon and Schuster Publishers, 1966.
Other thoughts on love, marriage and divorce.
126 pp.
$3.00

Cockain.
Divorce and Matrimonial Causes. London: Sweet and Maxwell, 1967.
£0.52½

Davis, Alice Jane.
Marriage and Divorce. Albany, New York:
National Institute of Municipal Clerks, 1956.
17 pp.

Dew.
Divorce Law and Practice. London: The Law Society, 1969.
Refresher lecture.

Deye, Raymond.
How to Beat the Divorce Racket. New York: Vantage Press, 1970.

Diamond, Milton.
So You Want a New Jersey Divorce. Dallas: 1957.
127 pp.

Finlay, H.A.
Divorce, Society and the Law. London: Butterworth Publishers, 1969.
127 pp.

Forbes.
Divorce Law. London: MacDonald and Evans, 1970.
200 pp.
£0.60

Gilzean, Elizabeth.
Why Do Marriages Fail? New York: Bantam Books,
50 cents

Glick, Paul C., and Arthur J. Norton.
Perspectives on the Recent Upturn in Divorce and Remarriage. Washington, D.C.: U.S. Department of Commerce Printing Office, 1972.
16 pp.

Greeley, Horace and Robert D. Owens.
Love, Marriage and Divorce and the Sovereignty of the Individual. New York: Collector's Editions, LTD., reprint 1971
$10.50

Hadley, Lila.
The Plight of the Single Parent. New York: J.P. Lippincott, 1972.

Hendler, Max.
Matrimonial Practices in the New York Supreme Court. New York: The Practicing Law Institute, 1966.

With analysis of the 1966 revision of the Domestic Relations Law, by Philip A. Schaeffer.
231 pp.

Herr, Dougal.
Marriage, Divorce and Separation. Newark, N.J.: Soney and Sage Co., 1963.

Hirsch, Barbara B.
Divorce: What a Woman Needs to Know.
Chicago, Ill.: Henry Regnery Company, 1972.
$6.95

Huff, Richard Maurice.
Resumé of Marriage and Divorce Laws of Oklahoma.
Oklahoma City: Oklahoma State Library, 1960.
41 p.

Ilch, Kenneth.
So You Want a Divorce. Las Vegas, Nev.: Fremont Publications, 1957.
122 pp.

Johannes, Jack.
Forms for Divorce and Annulment Under Family Code. Austin, Texas: 1970.
In cooperation with the Family Law Section of the State Bar of Texas.

Koffend, John B.
Letter to My Wife. New York: Saturday Review Press, 1972.
218 pp.

Koopman, Linda.
The Family and Divorce. Ithaca, New York: Sociological Resources of Secondary Schools, 1966.
90 pp

Krantzler, Mel.
Creative Divorce: A New Opportunity for Personal Growth. Philadelphia: J.B. Lippincott Company, 1974.
$6.95

Kronby, M.C.
Divorce Practice Manual. Toronto: Butterworth Pub. Co., 1969.
221 pp.
$12.75

Levy, J.
Uniform Marriage and Divorce Legislation: A Preliminary Analysis. New York: Dennis and Company,

Lindey, Alexander.
How to Use Separation Agreements: Ante-nuptial Contracts; Out of State Divorce. Revised edition.Albany, New York: Matthew Bender and Co., 1967.

Mariano, John Horace.
The Case Study Method in Psychoanalytic Legal Aid. New York: The Council on Marriage Relations, 1958.

Mariano, John Horace.
The Use of Psychotherapy in Divorce and Separation Causes. New York: The American Press, 1958.
179 pp.

Marriage and Divorce Law of Malawi.
London: Sweet and Maxwell, Ltd., 1970.
Restatement of African Law.
£3.90

McGuinness and O'Connor.
Divorce and Family Law, With Test Questions. London: Sweet and Maxwell, 1971.
£0.75

Moody, Lester Deane.
John Milton's Pamphlets on Divorce. Ann Arbor, Michigan: University Microfilms, 1957.

Moore, Arthur E.
Marriage, Divorce and Separation; With Forms. 2nd Edition. St. Paul: West Publishing Company, 1965. Vol.2.
Kept up to date by cumulative pocket supplements.

Nichols, Cicely.
Married Woman's Liberation Book. New York: Popular Library, 1972.
95 cents

Paget, Norman W., and Marcella R. Kern.
Counseling Services to Parents and Childern Involved in Divorce Proceedings. San Bernardino, California: 1960.
80 pp. Illus.

Passingham.
Divorce Reform Act. London: Butterworth Publishing Company, 1970.
£1.25

Phelps, Arthur Warren.
Divorce and Alimony in Virginia and West Virginia. Charlottesville: Michie Company, 1963.
557 pp.

Pineo, Peter Camden.
Dyadic and Change Analysis in a Study of Marriage and Divorce. Chicago: University of Chicago Library, Dept. of Photoduplication, 1960.

Quattrocchi, John.
Pitfalls in Marriage and Divorce. New York: Vantage Press, 1966 and 1967.
148 pp.

Rayden.
Practice and Law of Divorce. London: Butterworth and Company, 1970.
£17.50

Rees, D.P.
Divorce Handbook. London: Butterworth and Company, 1963.
£1.75

Report to the Governor and Legislature.
New Jersey Divorce Law Study Commission. Trenton, N.J.: 1970.
142 pp.

Commission on the Law. Marriage and Divorce. London: Irish University Press, 1969.

Reports of the Commission on the Law of Marriage and Divorce, and on the Marriage of British Subjects in Foreign countries, etc.
£31.65

Samuels, Aaron D.
Family Court Law and Practice. Revised edition. New York: Clark Boardman Publishers, 1972.
735 pp. Looseleaf
$30.00

Selts, Nathaniel C.
The Truth About Florida Divorce. Tampa, Fla.: Montgomery Pub., 1955.
30 pp.

Shaner, Donald W.
A Christian View of Divorce. Leiden, Netherlands: E.J. Brill, 1969.
115 pp.

Sheresky, Norman, and Mannes.
Uncoupling: The Art of Coming Apart. New York: Viking Press, Inc., 1972.
$6.95

Taft, Robert S.
Drafting Matrimonial Agreements and Property Settlements. 2nd ed. New York: Practicing Law Institute, 1971.
160 pp.

Taubes, Susan.
Divorcing. New York: Popular Library, 1972.
95 cents

Trimble, Benson.
Tennessee Divorce Authorities. Charlottesville, Va.: Michie Company,
637 pp.

Thant, General U.
Dissolution of Marriage, Annulment of Marriage and Judicial Separation. 1963.
105 pp.

Wenke, Robert A.
Marital Settlement Agreement. Los Angeles, California: Richter Law Book Company, 1969.
208 pp.

White, James L.
Divorce Proceedings.
University of South Dakota Press, 1972.
$1.95

Wingo, Earle L.
Mississippi Law of Divorce, Annulment, Separate Maintenance, Child Support and Custody, and Amended Adoption Laws. Hattiesburg, Miss.: 1957.
227 pp.

Winnett.
Church and Divorce. London: Mowbray House Publishing Company, 1968.
£o.52½

Adler, Felix.
Marriage and Divorce. New York: Appleton, 1915.
The three addresses were delivered before the Society of ethical culture of New York City; the first two were published 1905 under the title of Marriage and Divorce.
91 pp. NYPL

Alexander, Paul W. and others.
Conference on Divorce. Chicago: University of Chicago, 1952.
90 pp. ED

Amos, John Wesley.
Divorce Law (New Jersey) as enunciated by the Court. 1931
Compilation of Court Cases.

Apstein, Theodore E.
The Parting of the Ways: An Exposé of America's Divorce Tangle. New York: Dodge Publishing Co., 1935.
272 pp. SUNYA
ED

Archibald, William Charles.
The Divorce Remedy. Boston, Mass.: William Charles Archibald, 1910.
36 pp. NYPL

Bacal, Jacques, and Louise Sloane.
ABC of Divorce. New York: E. P. Dutton & Co. Inc., 1947.
128 pp.

Bartlett, George Arthur.
Men, Women and Conflict. New York: G. P. Putnam's Sons,
An intimate study of love, marriage, divorce.
294 pp. SUNYA

Bates, L. T.
Divorce and Separation of Aliens in France. New York:
ED

Bergler, Edmund.
Divorce Won't Help. New York: Harper, 1948.
240 pp. NYPL

Bernard, Jessie.
Remarriage: A Study of Marriage. New York: Dryden Press, 1956.

Bayly, Charles Bertrand.
Tax Manual for Divorce and Separation. Albany: Newkirk Associates, 1953.
219 pp. ED

Bishop, Joel P.
Commentaries on the Law of Marriage and Divorce. Boston, Mass.: Little, Brown & Co., 1881.
Miami
Law Library

Bossard, J. C.
Law Practice And Procedure

in Divorce as Applied in Pennsylvania, with Forms of Pleadings. New York: 1922.
ED

Bourne, G.
Marriage Indissoluble and Divorce Unscriptural. Harrisonburg, Va.: Davidson & Bourne, 1813.
114 pp., il., 64 p., 16°. NYPL

Brown, William Thurston.
The Moral Basis of the Demand for Free Divorce. Portland, Oregon: The Modern School, Love and Marriage Series 1861,
32 pp. NYPL

Bruce, Gustav Marius.
Marriage and Divorce, a Sociological and Theological Study. Minneapolis, Minn.: Augsburg Publishing House, 1930.
200 pp. NYPL

Buchanan, Edgar Simmons.
Christ's Teaching on Divorce According to the Earliest MSS., New York: 1915.
16 pp. NYPL

Bullen, Brian Cowling.
Love, Marriage and Divorce, and the Greatest of These Reformations! New York: J. S. Ogilive Pub. Co., 1912.
96 pp. NYPL

Carson, James M.
Law of Family, Marriage and Divorce in Florida, with Forms. Atlanta, Georgia: 1950.
Includes 1964 Pocket Supplement.

Carson, William English.
The Marriage Revolt. New York: Hearst's International Library Co., 1915.
A Study of Marriage and Divorce.
481 pp. NYPL

Chesterton, Gilbert Keith.
The Superstition of Divorce. New York: John Lane Company, 1920.
Reprinted in part from the New Witness.
150 pp. NYPL

Child, Francis.
Law of Divorce in New Jersey, with Procedure and Forms. Newark, New Jersey: 1929.
ED

Cirlot, Felix L.
Christ and Divorce. Lexington, Ky.: Trafton Publishing Co., 1945.
237 pp. NYPL

Colcord, Joanna C.
Broken Homes. New York: Russell Sage Foundation,

Corrance, Henry C.
The Church and Divorce. Con-

dord: International Journal of Ethics, 1919.
497 pp. NYPL

Coudert, F. R.
Marriage and Divorce Laws in Europe: A Study in Comparative Legislation. New York: Columbia University, 1893.
Thesis
108 pp. SUNYA
ED

Cowley, Charles.
Famous Divorces of All Ages. Lowell, Mass.: 1878.
ED

Cummings, Joseph.
Marriage and Divorce Laws of Massachusetts, with Forms. Somerville, Mass.: 1937.
ED

Curtis, Leslie.
Reno Reveries. Reno, Nevada: C. E. Weck, distributing agent, 1912.
95 pp. NYPL

Davis, Alice Jane.
Marriage and Divorce. National Institution of Municipal Clerks, 1956.
17 pp.

Davis, Milton L.
The Other Side of Divorce. Boston, Mass.: R. G. Badger, 1930
In the interest of those in the bondage of unhappy marriage.
141 pp. NYPL

Denning, A. T.
The Divorce Laws. Churchman Publishing Co., 1947.

Deutsch, Samuel and Simon Balicer.
How to Prove a Prima Facie Case. New York: 1928.
Contains "Grounds for Divorce in the Various States and Territories of the U.S.."

De Vecchi, Daolo.
A Discourse on Divorce and Its Shameful Abuse: A Disgrace to Civilization and a Danger to the Stability of a Government. New York: Private print., 1928.
68 pp. NYPL

Dix. D. D.
Divorce and Remarriage. New York: E. S. Gorham, 1902.
A sermon preached March 16, 1902.
18 pp. NYPL

Donovan, Joseph Mitchell.
The Law of Marriage, Annulment, Domicile, Divorce. Sioux Falls, S.D.: 1911.
100 pp. ED

Donovan, Joseph Mitchell.
The Law of Marriage, Annulment, Domicile, Divorce. S. Dakota: 1915.

Drummond, Isabel.
Getting A Divorce. New York: 1931.
Contains compilations of State Statutes.
163 pp. ED

Edwards & Co., E. B.
Information on the Divorce Laws of Massachusetts. Boston, 1879.

Edwards, George J. Jr.
Divorce: Its Development in Pennsylvania and the Present Law and Practice Therein. New York: Clark Boardman Co. Ltd., 1930.

Erkenbrach, Jennie E.
Appellant v. George A. Erkenbrach. New York: New York State Court of Appeals,
Opinion in a divorce case which contains a history of the statutory development of Divorce and Alimony in New York State.

Fisher, Hunter W.
The Divorce Problem. Waynesboro, Pa.: MacNeish Publishers, 1952.
Book presents opposite view of "Divorce & The Bible" by Donald Nurbie.

Foster, Henry H.
The Divorce Reform Law. Rochester, N. Y.: Cooperative Pub. Co., 1970.
66 pp.

Foster, Henry H., Barbara Flicker, and Matt Mederios.
New York Matrimonial Actions. New York: Practicing Law Inst.
316 pp.

Fuller, E. Dean.
Divorce Law in Mexico. New York: 1942.
30 pp. ED

Gigot, Francis.
Christ's Teaching Concerning Divorce. New York: Bensiger Brothers, 1912.

Glick, Paul C., and Arthur J. Norton.
Perspectives on the Recent Upturn in Divorce and Remarriage. Washington, D.C.: U. S. Department of Commerce Printing Office, 1972.
16 pp.

Gore, Charles.
The Question of Divorce. New York: Charles Scribner's Sons, 1911.

Griswald, R. W.
Doctrine and Discipline of Divorce. Philadelphia: John W. Moore, 1847.

Gwynne, Rev. Walter.
Divorce in American Under State and Church. New York: The Macmillan Co., 1925.
154 pp. SUNY

Hambledon, Phyllis.
Nobody's Child.
1951.

Herr, Dougal.
Law of Marriage, Divorce and Separation in New Jersey . . . with Forms. Hoboken, New Jersey: 1938.
ED

Hirsh, Hugo.
Hirsh's Tabulated Digest of the Divorce Laws of the United States. New York: 1901.
ED

Helmes, John H.
Marriage and Divorce. New York: B. W. Heubsch, 1913.

Horowitz, Jacob Israel.
Manual of Divorce and Other Matrimonial Actions. New York: Central Book Co.,
450 pp.

Hudgings, Franklyn.
Law of Marriage and Divorce: A Digest and Analysis of all States . . . also Mexico, Cuba, Canada, England and France. New York: 1935.
68 pp. ED

Hull, William.
Law of Marriage and Divorce: A Lecture. New York: Hartwick Seminary,
18 pp. ED

Indovina, F. J., and J. E. Dalton.
Statutes of all States and Territories with Annotations on Marriage, Annulment, and Divorce. Santa Monica, Calif.:,
ED

Ireland, Gordon.
Divorce in the Americas. Buffalo, N. Y.: Dennis & Company, Inc., 1947.
306 pp. ED

Johnson, Julia E.
Selected Articles on Marriage and Divorce. New York: H. W. Wilson Co., 1925.
293 pp. SUNYA

Joint State Government, General Assembly.
Proposed Marriage and Divorce Codes for Pennsylvania. Harrisburg, Pa.: 1961.
134 pp.

Keezer. Frank H.
A Treatise on the Law of Marriage and Divorce. Indianapolis, Ind.: The Bobbs-Merrill Co., 1923.

Kirk, K. E.
Marriage and Divorce. Don Mills, Ont.: Hodder & Stoughton, 1948.

Klein, R. H.
Pennsylvania Law and

Procedure. Philadelphia: 1937.
1118 pp. ED

Kuchler, F. W. H.
Law of Marriage and Divorce Simplified. Dobbs Ferry, N. Y.: Oceana Publications, 1961.

Lawerence, William H.
Law of Divorce and Annulment of Marriage in Maryland. Baltimore, Md.: 1939.
60 pp. ED

Lichtenberger, James P.
Divorce, A Social Interpretation. New York: McGraw Hill, 1931.

Lindauer, Louis.
Forms and Procedures in Matrimonial Cases. Brooklyn, New York: 1948.
A desk book for lawyers, law clerks, and law students.
145 pp. ED

Lindey, Alexander.
Separation Agreements Ante-Nuptial Contracts: Their Preparation, Execution, Operation, Interpretation and Enforcement and the Role They Play in Judicial Separation and Divorce. Albany, New York: M. Bender and Co., Inc., 1937.

Lloyd, A. P.
Law of Divorce. Boston, Mass.: 1887.
Compilation of the latest divorce statistics.
ED

Lombard, John P.
Marriage and Divorce of Massachusetts. Boston, Mass.: Boston Law Book Co., 1949.
A modern treatise on marriage, divorce, separate support, and annulment including practice and procedure with forms based upon prior editions of Joseph Cummings.
ED

Luckock, Herbert Mortimer.
The History of Marriage, Jewish and Christian, in Relation to Divorce and Certain Forbidden Degrees. New York: Longmans, Green & Co., 1895.
359 pp. SUNYA

Mackay, Richard Vance.
Law of Marriage and Divorce Simplified. Dobbs Ferry, N. Y.: Oceana Publications, 1959.
Legal Almanac Series.
96 pp.

Mahon, Thomas.
The Church and Divorce. St. Louis, Mo.: B. Herder, 1926.
73 pp. SUNYA

Mariano, John Horace.
A Psychoanalytic Lawyer Looks at Marriage and Divorce. New York: The Council

on Marriage Relations, 1952.
176 pp.

Marshall, Leon C., and Geoffrey May.
The Divorce Court. Baltimore, Md.: John Hopkins Press, 1932.
159 pp.

May, Geoffrey.
Divorce Law in Maryland. Baltimore, Md.: 1932.
Study of the judicial system in Maryland.
53 pp. ED

May, Geoffrey.
Divorce Law in Ohio. Baltimore, Md.: 1932.
Study of judicial administration in Ohio.
76 pp. ED

Mielziner, M.
The Jewish Law of Marriage and Divorce. New York: Block Printing Co., 1901.

Morland, John W.
Keezer on the Law of Marriage and Divorce. Indianapolis, Ind.: Bobbs-Merrill, 1948.

Nelson, W. T.
Divorce and Annulment. 1945.
Legal textbook.

Nelson, William O.
Nelson on Divorce and Annulment. Chicago, Ill.: Callaghan & Co., 1945.

Phaff, Roger Alton.
Family Law and Marital Reconciliation Procedures in Europe. Chicago, Ill.: 1966.
12 pp.

Pollitti, Basil Hubbard.
Justice and the Justices. Daytona Beach, Fla.: College Pub. Co., 1954.
210 pp.

Power, James G.
Marriage and Divorce. New York: American News Co., 1870.

Ralli, Paul.
Nevada Lawyer. Dallas, Texas: Mathis, Van Nort & Co., 1946.
152 pp.

Ringrose, Hyacinth.
Marriage and Divorce Law of the World. New York: Musson-Draper, 1911.
270 pp.

Ringwalt, Ralph Curtis.
Divorce Bibliography. New York: 1905.
201 pp.

Rogers, Anna B.
Why American Marriages Fail. Boston, Mass.: Houghton-Mifflin, 1909.

Russell, Bertrand, Fannie Hurst, H.G. Wells, and others.

Divorce. New York: The John Day Co., 1930.
92 pp.

Siegel, David D.
Commentary on the Domestic Relations Law. Brooklyn, N.Y.: E. Thompson, 1964.
98 pp.

Simak, A.
Legal and Ethical Considerations of Mexican Divorces. 1964.

Slade, Frances.
Divorce if You Must. New York: Coward-McCann, Inc., 1938.
165 pp.

Smith, Stevenson, M.W. Wilkinson, and L.C. Wagoner.
A summary of the Laws of the Several States Governing: Washington University Bulletin, 83, 1914.
87 pp.

Snyder, W.L.
The Geography of Marriage. N.Y.: 1889.

Spellman, Howard Hilton.
Successful Management of Matrimonial Causes. Englewood Cliffs, N.J.: Prentice-Hall, 1954.
306 pp.

Stern, William Bernhard.
Mexican Marriages and Divorce. San Diego, Calif.: San Diego Offset Print Co., 1952.
18 pp.

U.S. Bureau of the Census.
Marriage and Divorce, Annual Report, 1922, 1932. Washington, D.C.: Government Printing Office, 1932.

U.S. Bureau of the Census.
Report on Marriage and Divorce, 1867 to 1916. Washington, D.C.: Government Printing Office, 1916.

U.S. Bureau of the Census.
Report on Marriage and Divorce, 1916. Washington, D.C.: Government Printing Office, 1916.

U.S. Bureau of the Census.
A Review of Marriage and Divorce Statistics, 1887 to 1937. Washington, D.C.: Government Printing Office, 1937.

U.S. National Center for Health Statistics.
Marriage and Divorce Registration in the U.S.. Washington, D.C.: U.S.Dept. of Health, Education and Welfare, 1966.
23 pp.

Virtue, Maxine Boord.
Family Cases in Court. Dur-

ham, N.C.: Duke University Press, 1956.
Prepared for the Interprofessional Commission on Marriage and Divorce Laws.
290 pp.

Vreeland, Hamilton.
Validity of Foreign Divorces. Chicago: 1938.
A study concerning the extraterritorial recognition of divorce decrees.

Warren, Oscar LeRoy.
Schouler Divorce Manual. Albany, New York. 1944.
Contains Statutes of the states summarized.

White, Frederick A.
Laws on Marriage, Divorce and Property Rights of Married Women of All States and Alaska, Hawaii, Arizona, New Mexico and the District of Columbia, with Citations to Laws by Chapter and Section. Los Angeles, Calif.: Baumgardt Publications, 1910.
423 pp.

Whiting, Henry C.
Marriage and Divorce. New York: John Potter, 1894.
377 pp.

Willock, James Henry.
The Florida Law of Divorce. Miami, Florida. 1941.
47 pp.

Wilner, Charles.
Alimony: The American Tragedy. New York: Vantage Press, 1952.
329 pp.

Woolsey, T.D.
An Essay on Divorce Legislation. New York: Scribner's, 1869.

Woolsey, T.D.
Divorce and Divorce Legislation Especially in the United States. 1882.

An Essay on Marriage: or The Lawfulness of Divorce, in Certain Cases Considered.
Addressed to the feelings of mankind. Philadelphia, Pa.: Zachariah Poulson Jr., 1788.
28 p. NYPL

New York Public Library Divorce Bibliography. New York: 1905.
List of works in the New York Public Library relating to marriage and divorce.
48 pp. NYPL

New York State Legislature. Joint Committee on Matrimonial and Family Laws. Albany, New York. 1956/57.
Issues in the series of Legislative documents.

United States Judiciary Committee References on Divorce.

Washington, D. C.: Gov. Printing Office, 1915.

List of references submitted to the Committee on the Judiciary, United States Senate, Sixty-third Congress, third session, in connection with S. J. Res. 109, a resolution proposing on amendment to the constitution of the U. S. relating to divorces. Prepared under the direction of Hermann H. B. Meyer, Chief Bibliographer, Library of Congress, Washington, D. C.
110 pp. NYPL

PUBLICATIONS ON DIVORCE (Worldwide)

ARGENTINA

Barroetauena, Diego Lucio El Divorcio en el derecho Argentino. Buenos Aires: La Ley, 1967.
260 pp. SUNY

Barroetauena, Diego Lucio
Divorcio Reforma civil y Procesal. Buenos Aires: La Ley, 1968.
258 pp. SUNY

Bas, Arturo M.
El cancer de la sociedad. Buenos Aires: S. de Amorrortu, 1932.
255 pp.

Camara, Arruda.
A familia eo divorcio; Conferencia proferida na sessao plenaria do. "Congresso do Esea pulario", no Recife, Rio De Janeiro, 1951.
42 pp. NYPL

Corcao, Gustavo.
Claro escuro; ensalos sobre casamente, divorcio, Amor, sexo e outros assuntos. Rio de Janeiro: Agir, 1960.
227 pp. NYPL

Goyend, Copello, Hector R
Divorcio por mutuo consentintimiento. Buenos Aires: Edicoines Patrium, 1969.
35 pp. NYPL

Viale, Carlos Dalmiro.
Buenos Aires 1902: "Batalla del Divorcio". Buenos Aires: Poder, 1957.
235 pp. SUNY

COMMONWEALTH OF AUSTRALIA

Conference for Solicitors and Accountants
Dubbo: 1966
Strata titles and divorce as related to property settlements; two papers presented at the conference for solicitors and accountants, at Dubbo, Sept. 1966.
52 pp. NYPL

New South Wales Humanist Society.
Marriage and Divorce. Sydney: 1970
15 pp. NYPL

Stephen, Sir Alfred.
Australian Divorce Bills; the Objections Raised to Them, Religious and Social, Considered. Sidney: 1888.

BRAZIL

Barbosa, Ruy.
O divorcio e o anarchismo; prefacio e revisao de Homero Pires. Rio de Janeiro: Editora Guanabara, 1933.
200 pp. NYPL

Prunes, Lourence Mario.
psbtica do desouite amigauel.

Sao Paulo: Sugestoes Literias, 1970.
175 pp. NYPL

CANADA

Cartwright, Henry L.
Law and Practice in Divorce and Matrimonial Causes in Ontario." Toronto: 1934.
174 pp. ED

Cartwright, H.L., and E.R. Lovekin.
The Law and Practice of Divorce in Canada. Toronto: Canada Law Book Co., 1962.
517 pp.

Champagne, Pierre A.
La cruaute mentale, seule cause du divorce? Montreal: Editions de l'Homme, 1971.
159 pp. NYPL

Chapman, Frederick Aurel R.
Law and Marriage. New York: McGraw-Hill, 1968.
163 pp.

Evans, R. R.
Law and Practice Relating to Divorce and Other Matrimonial Causes (in Canada), Calgary: 1923.

Gemmill, John Alexander.
The practice of the Parliament of Canada upon Bills of Divorce including a Historical Sketch of Parliamentary Divorce and Summaries of All the Bills of Divorce Presented to Parliament from 1867–1888, also Notes on the Provincial Divorce Courts. Toronto: Carswell & Co., 1889.
ED

Heaton, S. Lewell.
Divorce Manual (for Ontario, Canada). Hamilton, 1945.
A five year digest of the more important cases . . . 1939–1944.
ED

Hogg, F. D.
Parliamentary Divorce Practice in Canada. Toronto: 1925.
ED

MacDonald, James. C. and Lee K. Ferrier.
Canadian Divorce Law and Practice. Toronto: Carswell, 1969.
NYPL

Ontario Law Reform Commission.
Report of the Ontario Law Reform Commission to the Attorney General for Ontario on Certain Aspects of the Proposed Divorce Legislation Contained in Bill C-187 1968. Toronto: Dept. of the Attorney General, 1968.
10 pp. NYPL

CEYLON

Jayewardene, C.E.
The Roman-Dutch Law of Divorce, with Special Reference to Ceylon. Colombo: Columbo Apothecaries' Co., 1952
126 pp. ED

CUBA

Dumas, Alexandre. the younger.
La Cuestion de Divorce.
La Habana, Soc. editorial Cuba Contemporanca, 1918.
229 pp. NYPL

DENMARK

Budtz, Hanne.
Æ gteskab, separation, skilsmisse. København, Idag, 1969.
112 pp. NYPL

EGYPT

Al-Bindari, 'Abd al-Wahhab
1969.
214 pp. NYPL

EUROPE

Cohn, Herman.
Foreign laws of Marriage and Divorce. Countries of European Continent, 1937. (comp. pt. 1)

Doroghi, Ervin.
Grounds for Divorce in European Countries. New York: Research Division of the New School, 1955. Research Div. of the New School for Social Research. Occasional papers.
51 pp.

Koopman, M.W.E.
Het nieuwe echtscheidingsrecht. Zwolk: Tjeenk Willink, 1971.
81 pp. NYPL

FINLAND

Lainualmistelukunta.
Forslag till regeringens proposition-till riksdagen angaende andring av vissa stadganden om aktenskaps in -guenda och upplosning sant dartill anslutaa bestammelser. Helsingfors: 1968.
23 pp. NYPL

FRANCE

Ami (L') des enfans.
Motion en faveur du divorce. Paris: Devaux, 1782?
8 pp. NYPL

Barruel, Augustin de.
Lettres sur le divorce, á un député de l' Assembleé nationale, par l'abbe de barruel; ou bien, Réfutation d'un ouvrage ayant pour titre: Du divorce. Paris: Chez Crapart, 1789.
36,42 pp. NYPL

Bellée, Paul.
Du divorce au mariage, divorce et union libre, idée chrétienne du mariage, le foyer chrétien; conferences donnes a Notre-Dame de Bon-Secours de Trovcille et á Saint-Louis d'Antin. Paris: A. Roblot, 1913.
268 pp. NYPL

Bertillon, J.
Etude demographique du divorce et de la séparation de corps dans les différents pays de l' Europe. Paris: G. Masson, 1883.
178 pp. NYPL

Bolo, H.
Du mariage au divorce. Paris: R. Haton, 1896.
277 pp. NYPL

Bonsirven, Joseph.
Le Divorce Dans Le Nouveau Testament. Paris: Desclee et Cie, 1948.
NYPL

Cauviere, J.
Le divorce au puint de vue Catholique & Social. Paris: J. Gainche, 1897.
6 pp. NYPL

Cayle, Abbé.
Smille et divorce. Paris: Bloud & Cic, 1908.
61 pp. NYPL

Coanec, Somone.
Les Prublemes du divorce. Paris: R. Laffant, 1970.
331 pp. NYPL

Coudert, Frederic René.
De Divorce. Reponse A M. Dumas. New York: Courrier des Etats Unis, 1880.
59 pp. NYPL

Coulon, Henri.
Le' divorce et la separation de corps. Paris: 1890–'97.
ED

Coulon, Henri.
Le divorce par consentement mutuel isa necessité-sa moralité; suivi d'un projet de loi. Paris: Marchal & Billard, 1902.
137 pp. NYPL

Couton, Henri and R.De Chauagnes
LeMariage et le divorce de demain. Paris: E. Flammarion, 1908.
432 pp. NYPL

Descotes, Adolphe.
Le divorce par consentement mutuel. Un chaptiture de morale et d Legislation Sociale. Paris: F. Leva, 1904.
30 pp. NYPL

Dessaulles, L. A.
Les erreurs de L'eglise en droit naturel et canonique sur le mariage et le divorce. Paris: A. Pedone, 1894.

Dumas, Alexandre, the younger.
La Question du Divorce. Paris: C. Levy, 1880.
317 pp. NYPL

Holstein-Brunswic, Collette.
Le droit et l'amour, Paris:

Flammarien, 1970.
235 pp. NYPL

Kato, Kazuyashi.
Provisional Measures in French Divorce 1922.
147 pp. NYPL

Leclercq, Michel.
Le divorce et Église: le mariage est-il toujours indissolube? Paris: Fayard, 1969.
156 pp. NYPL

Libmann, Jeam.
Le divorce. Tournai: Casterman, 1971.
162 pp.

Rodiere, Jean.
Le divorce et la separation de corps. Paris: Europa, 1969.
157 pp. NYPL

Voulet, Jacques.
Toutes les questions pratigues sur le divorce et le séparation de corps. Paris: J. Delmas et Cic, 1970.
NYPL

Divorce—sanction et divorce faillite en droit compare francais et allemand, actes de latable ronde d. 24 aveil. Paris: Dalloz, 1969.
123 pp. NYPL

GERMAN REPUBLIC

David, Jakob.
Wie unaufloslich ist die ehe? Eine Dokumentation. Hrsg. von Jakob David und Franz Schmalz. Ascheffenburg: Pattloch, 1969.
373 pp. NYPL

Luderitz, Alexander.
Empfiehlt es sich, Gründe und Folgen der Ehescheidung neu zu regeln: Gutachten, Munchen: Beck, 1970.
122 pp. NYPL

Schmidt, Gerhard.
Welchen Einfluss hat die Scheidung eines ehegatten auf der zu seinenounsten abgeschbossenen Lebensversich-crungsvertrag?. Marburg: 1967.
99 pp. NYPL

Toop, Hans.
Divorce Bibliography.
Borna-Leipzig: F. Noske, 1908.
*Ehescheidung and Aufhebung der ehelichen Gemeinschaft nach dem Burgerlichen Gesetzbuch.
56 pp. NYPL

Weil, Norman.
Zum Thema Ehescheidung. Stuttgart: Verl. Katholisches Bibelwerk, 1970.
110 pp. NYPL

Werner, Nikolaus.
Ehestorung und Gattenrecht. Bonn. 1968.
175 pp. NYPL

Wolf, Ernst.
Eheverfehlung, ehezerruhung und einverstandliche scheindung in den vorschlagen zur Reform des Ehescheidungrechts in England. Hrsg. von Ernst Wolf, Ubers, und erlauherd Luke Eingeleitet von Ernst Wolf, Ubers und Grlautert von Dietmar Seiler. Müenchen: Heymann, 1969.
113 pp. NYPL

Deutscher Juristentag. Zivilrechtliche Abteiling.
Empfiehlt es sich, grunde und folgen der Chescheidung nuu zu regeln? Munchen Beck. 1970.
4 pp. NYPL

GREAT BRITAIN

Ali, Muhammad Maulana.
Divorce in Islam.
Woking, Woking Muslim Mission & Literary Trust, 1875.
24 pp. ED

Bartlett, George Arthur.
Men, Women and Conflict; An Intimate Study of Love, Marriage and Divorce. London: G. P. Putnam's Sons, 1931.
4 pp. NYPL

Binney, Cecil.
The Divorce Court: Gt. Britain High Court of Justice. London: Probate, Divorce & Admiralty Division, 1957.
157 pp.

Box, G. H., and Charles Gove.
Divorce in the New Testament. London: S.P.C.K., 1921.

Brooks, Leslie.
"Matrimonia causes . . . the Matrimonia causes Act, 1937: the summary procedure (domestic procedings) Act. London: 1937.
ED

Browne, George, William Lately and D.P. Rees.
"Brown and Latey's Law and practice in divorce and matrimonial causes", London: 1931.
ED

Bull, Paul Bertie.
Marriage and Divorce. London: Society for Promoting Christian Knowledge, 1924.

Butzer, Martin.
London: Authoritie, 1644.
The judgment of Martin Bucer, concerning divorce writt'n to Edward the Sixth, in his second book of the Kingdom of Christ. And now English. Wherein a late book restoring the doctrine and discipline of divorce, is here

confirm'd and justify'd by the authoritie of Martin Bucer, to the Parliament of England.
NYPL

Charles, R. H.
The Teaching of the New Testament on Divorce. London: Williams & Norgate, 1921.

Charles, Robert Henry.
Divorce and the Roman Dogma Nullity. Edinburgh: T & T. Clark, 1927.
100 pp. NYPL

Chase, F. N.
What did Christ Teach About Divorce? London: S.P.C.K. 1921.

Chesterton, Gilbert Keith.
Divorce Versus Democracy. London: Soc. of S.S. Peter & Paul, 1916. Reprinted from "Nash's Magazine."
13 pp. NYPL

Chesterton, Gilbert Keith.
The Superstition of Divorce., London: Chatto & Windus, 1920.
"The earlier part of this book came out in the form of five articals which appeared in the New Witness."
NYPL

Collington, B.A.
Lushington's Summary Jurisdiction Separation and Maintenance Acts 1895–1925, London. 1929.
ED

Coutts, John W.
The Church and the Sex Question. London: J. Clarke & Company, Ltd., 1926(?)
NYPL

Darwin, Leonard.
Divorce and Illegitimacy. London: Eugenics Education Soc., 1918.
11 pp. NYPL

Dawson, W.J.E.
The Christian Attitude to Divorce. London, (Church quarterly review), 1938.
NYPL

Dew, E.R.
Divorce Law and Practice. London: 1969.
Refresher lecture delivered in 1968 and earlier years.
30 pp.

Dixon, W.J.
Law and Practice in Divorce and Other Matrimonial Causes. London: 1908
NYSED

Fellows, Alfred.
The Case Against the English Divorce Law. London: 1932
ED

Fenn, Henry Edwin.
Thirty-five Years in the Divorce Court. Boston: Little Brown, 1911.
309 pp.

Ford, D.M.
Marriage, Divorce and Separation. London: 1910.
ED

Grant, H.B.G.
Marriage, Separation and Divorce. London: Stevers & Sons Ltd., 1948.

Gribble, Francis Henry.
The Fight for Divorce.
London: Hurst & Blackett, 1932.
288 pp. ED

Hartley, C. G.
Divorce. London

Herbert, Alan Patrick.
The Ayes have it: The Story of the Marriage Bill.
London: Methuen & Co., Ltd., 1937.

Herbert, Alan Patrick.
The Right to Marry. London: Methuen, 1954.
79 pp.

Hermand, George Fergusson:
Lord Hermand's Consistorial Decisions. Edinburgh: Stair Society Publications, 1940.
164 pp. ED

Kelly, Edmond.
The French Law of Marriage: Marriage Contracts and Divorce and the Conflict of Laws Arising Therefrom., London: 1895.
ED

Kitchin, Shepherd Braithwaite.
A History of Divorce. London: Chapman & Hall, Ltd., 1912.
293 pp. ED

Laing, Margaret.
Woman on Woman. London: Sidgewick and Jackson, 1971.
228 pp. NYPL

Latey, William.
Jurisdiction and Recognition in Divorce and Nullity Decrees: The International Position (with a translation of parts of Spanish law and Civil divorce). London: International Law Association, 1933.
111 pp. ED

MacQueen, John.
Treatise on the Appellate Jurisdiction of the House of Lords and Privy Council. . . . with the Practice of the Parliamentary Divorce. London: 1842.

McGregor, Oliver Ross.
Divorce in England, a Centenary Study. London: Heinemann, 1957.
220 pp.

Palmer, Henry, and Patricia Marks.
A Guide to Divorce.
London: Bodley Head, 1965.
126 pp.

Passingham, Bernard.
Divorce Law and Practice. London: London Law Society, 1969.
NYPL

Rayden, William.
Rayden's Law and Practice in Divorce and Family Matters in the High Court, County Courts, and Magistrates' Courts. London: Butterworth, 1971.

Russell, Bertrand, Fannie Hurst, H.G. Wells, N. Douglas.
Divorce As I See It. London: The Daily Express, 1930 reprint.
92 pp. NYPL

Scott, George and Leslie Smith.
Women Alone. London: Elm Tree Books, 1971.
134 pp.

Shelford, Leonard.
Treatise of Law of Marriage and Divorce. Philadelphia: 1841.

Swift, Morris.
Jewish Marriage and Divorce, with a foreword by Israel Brodie. London: Beth Din, 1962.
Title also in Hebrew.
17 pp.

Tolstoy, D.
Divorce and Matrimonial Causes, with Matrimonial Causes and Rules. London: 1946.
ED

Marriage and Divorce: Studies in History and Jurisprudence. London: Oxford University Press, 1901.

Royal Commission on Marriage and Divorce. London: H. M. Stationery Office Report, 1951–1955, 1956.
Parliamentary papers by command.
404 pp.

Reform on the Grounds of Divorce—Law Commission. The field of choice: report on the reference under section 3 (1) (e) of the Law Commissions Act 1965, presented to Parliament by the Lord High Chancellor, London, H.M.S.O., 1967.
62 pp.

The cases of polygamy, concubinage, adultery, divorce, ec. seriously and learnedly discussed. Being a complete collection of all the remarkable tryals and tracts which have been written on those important subjects. By the most eminent

hands. London, Printed for T. Payne [ect.] 1732.
240 pp. NYPL

An answer to a book, entitled, The doctrine and Discipline of Divorce, or A Plea for Ladies and Gentlewomen, and All Other Married Women Against Divorce. Wherein both sexes are vindicated from all . . . mistakes whatsoever: and the unsound principles of the author are . . . confuted by authority of Holy Scripture, the laws of this land, and sound reason. London, Printed by G.N. for William Lee , 1644.
44 pp. NYPL

HUNGARY

Articales by Thirring, Gusnate, Etienne Bernat, and others. Divorce et Suicides. Leurs causes et les moyens de les combattre. Hungary: Enguete de La Société congroise de Statistique, 1927.
Preface by Dr. Desire Laky.
137 pp. Tables NYPL

INDIA

Jhabuala, Noshiruan Hormoji. Law of Marriage and Divorce in India. Bombay: D.B. Taraporeuala Sons, 1954.

A simple and concise guide for the layman dealing with the legal problems of engagement, marriage, and divorce, affecting Hindus, Muslims, Parsis and Christians.
11 pp.

Qudri, Anwar Ahnad. The Dissolution of Muslim Marriage Act. Lucknow: Eastern Book Company,
126 pp.

Sethi, Raghbirlal Bhagatram. Muslim Marriage and Its Dissolution. Ailahabad: Law Book Co., 1961

Being an exhaustive and critical exposition of Muslim Law of marriage and its dissolution with a commentary on the dissolution of the Muslim Marriage Act with up to date caselaw.
271 pp.

Bombay Hindu Divorce Act (Act No. XII of 1947) with rules made thereunder, and the Indian Divorce Act, the Parsi Marriage and Divorce Act, the Dissolution of Muslim Marriage Act, the Native Converts-Marriage Dissolution Act with exhaustive commentary and case laws by Bansilal H. Mehta, assisted by Mukundray M. Mehta. With a foreword by Himatal P. Shukla, Ahnedabad: C C Vora, 1949.
161 pp. NYPL

IRELAND

Irish University Press Series of British Parliamentary Papers. Marriage and Divorce. Shannon: Irish Univ. Press, 1969.
NYPL

ITALY

Ajcardi, Enrico.
Divorzio? Breui Considerazion: giuridiche e sociali intorno a questa istituzione. Roma: A. Befani, 1881.
106 pp. NYPL

Antonini, Giuseppe.
Il divorzio degli alienati; echi della vita A Mombello. Torino: Fratelli Bocca, 1923.
130 pp. NYPL

Ballerini (G-inseppa).
Matrimonio e Divorzio a Proposito dell' Attnale Progetto Ministeriale. Siena: S. Bernardino, 1903.
55 pp. NYPL

Barroetavena, Francisco Antonio.
Dos Conferencias del Dr. F.A. Barroetavena. El clericalismo y el Divorcio. Emancipacion Italina. El XX de septiembre, fraternidad y conflicto Italo-Argentino. Buenos Aires: Compana sud-America de billetes-de-benco, 1912.
51 pp. NYPL

Bartoli, A.
Del Divorzio. Firenze: A. Salami, 1891.
NYPL

Battisti, G.
Il Divorzio sotto Accusa? Pescara: Ferretti, 1969.
22 pp. NYPL

Belotti, Bortelo.
Politica del Costume (studie saggi).
Milano: Unita, 1924.
La legislazione italiana in rapporto al costume. Per i diritti della donna. Le ferme in parta e la fratta delle bianche. La disciplina del cinematografo. La repressione legislativa della pornografia. La questione del divorzio prima e dopa la guerra
240 pp. NYPL

Berenini, Agostino, and A. Ruffoni.
Il divorzio dinanzi alla camera. Milano: B. Bacchini, 1902.
110 pp. NYPL

Bernardo, Domenico di.
El divorzio considerate nella teoria e nella practica. Palemo: A. Natale, 1875.
807 pp. NYPL

Béze, Théodore de'.
Tractatio De Rupudiis Et Divortiis: In Qva leraeqve De cau-

sis matrimonialibus . . . incidentes controversiae ex verbo Dei deciduntur. Additur Juris Civilis Romanorum & veterum his de rebus nonum examen, ad eiusdem Verbi Dei, & aequitatis horman. Ex Th. Bezae. Praelectionibus in priorem ad Corinthios Epistolan. Genevae: Apud Eustathium Vignon, 1605.
256 pp. NYPL

Bommel, C.J. van.
*Dedivartio ex mutuo consensu. Trajecti ad Rhenum, 1821.
62 pp. NYPL

Bonavita, F.
La legge sur divorzio: spiegata al popolo.
Firenze: G. Nerbini, 1902.
28 pp. NYPL

Branchini, E. Giuseppe.
Pro Divorzio. Conferenza. Arezzo: F'lli Shat ti, 1902.
p. NYPL

Bronzini, C.
Studio sul Divorzio. Matera: F.P. Conti, 1899.
69 pp. NYPL

Calui, Carlo.
Ricerche sul Divorzio fra' Cristiani. Paula: G. Bolzani, 1790.
216 pp. NYPL

Cantessa, Lorenzo.
Divorcio ed uno Studio Critico e Protilattico del Matrimonio. Geneva: Tip.della Giovent'n, 1903.
21 pp. NYPL

Cappellazzi, A.
Il Divorzio: Piccolo Studio. Iodi: Tip. Uesci Quirico e Camagni, 1893.
246 pp. NYPL

Caronna, Nunzio.
Matrimonio e Divorzio. Napoli: N. Jovene & Co., 1903.
150 pp. NYPL

Ciaffi, Francesco.
Separazione e Divorzio? Subiaco: Tipografia Angelucci, 1886.
311 pp. NYPL

Cimbali, Enrico.
Due riforme urgenti il divorzio e la ricerca della paternitá naturale.
Torino: Unione tipografico-editrice, 1902.
73 pp. NYPL

Cipriani, Franco.
Da lla Separazione al Divorzio. Napoli: Jovene, 1971.
200 pp. NYPL

Colombo, Arrigo.
Proposte di un Cattolico per il Divorzio in Italia. Manduria:

Lacaita, 1970.
106 pp. NYPL

Colombo, Eugenio.
Perché Combattiamo il Divorzio. Milano: Volonteri & Co. 1920(?).
45 pp. NYPL

Fisichella, S. Francesco.
Il Divorzio: Observazion: Critche.
Messina: Carmelo de Stefano, 1894.
164 pp. NYPL

Francki Anna.
Il Divorzio e la Donna. Firenze: G. Nerbini, 1902.
Film reproduction. Reduction 12. positive.
28 pp. NYPL

Frederici, Emilio.
Divorzio e Socialismo. Venezia: Tipogr., Emiliana, 1902.
181 pp. NYPL

Genni, Enrico.
Il Divorzio Considerato Come contro Natura ed Antigiuridico. Napoli: F. Giannin, 1902.
122 pp. NYPL

Lombardi, Gabrio.
Divorzio, Referendum, Concordato. Bologna: Il Mulino, 1970.
182 pp. NYPL

Scritti, di Enrico Di Rovasenda, Mario Cicala, Giuseppe Olivero, Bernardo Merlo, Luisa Guarnero, Mario Longo, and Rodolfo Sacco.
L'Ora del Divorzia? Fireze: Vallecchi, 1969.
219 pp. NYPL

Carini, Spartaco.
Divorzio in Italia. Rome: Citta, 1969.
156 pp. NYPL

Palladino, Afonso.
Il Divorzio. Commento teorica-pratico alla legge sulla disciplina dei casi scioglimento del matrimonio. Milano: Giuffre, 1970.
366 pp. NYPL

Parca, Gabriella.
I Separati. Milano: 1969.
236 pp. NYPL

Pittau, Massimo.
Il Divorzio. Cagliari: 1968.
317 pp. NYPL

Radius, Emilio.
Storia del Matrimonio in Tutti i Temp: in Tutti i Paesi. Milano: Martello, 1971.
243 pp.. NYPL

Scazziocchio, Oscar.
Discorso sul Divorzio. Italia prigioniers. Svolgimento storico del matrimonia, con la ri-

produzione di alcuni importanti documenti . . . Roma: Julia, 1969.
23, 46 pp. Illus.
NYPL

Tanturri, Riccardo.
L'introduzione di Divorzio in Italia.
Napoli: 1970.
98 pp. NYPL

Unione giuristi cattolici Italiani Indissolubilita del matrimonioee referendum popolare. (Att: completi del xx Convegno nazionale di studio) Milano: Giuffré, Roma, Iustitia, 1970.
223 pp. NYPL

Van Aken, G. A.
De Divortio e Jusoue Effectibus ex Juris Romani et Hodierni Principiis. Lugduni: Batavorum, 1819.
86 pp. NYPL

JAPAN

Maruyama, Masaya.
"*Onna Kara Nige-dasu horitsu no hon,*" colophon inserted., 1969.
238 pp. NYPL

Ota Takeo.
Gendai no ricon monda. Includes bibliographical references.
4, 842 pp. NYPL

Tsubouchi, Yoshihiro. Rikon. A revision of Yoshihiro Tsubouchi's thesis. Bibliography: University of Kyoto,
231 pp. NYPL

KENYA

Commission on the Law of Marriage and Divorce. Report. Nairobi: Govt. Printers, 1968.
209 pp. NYPL

MEXICO

Faraon, Chaul y Freja, and Carmen Hened. El Divorcio. Mexico. 1959.
103 pp. NYPL

Gorocica, Sánchez Carlos.
Estudio e interpretacion de la fracción XI del artículo 267 del Código civil para ek Distrito y Territorios Federales. Mexico: 1966.
90 pp. NYPL

Haberman, Roberto.
The Divorce Laws of Mexico.
New York: 1930.
46 pp. ED

Júarez,Ocampo Roberto.
El Divorcio; Necesidad de Restrin-girlo. Mexico: 1959.
61 pp. NYPL

NETHERLANDS

Echtscheiding.
Samengesteld door M. Nevejan en J. Huijts. Bussum: Paul Brand, 1969.
223 pp. NYPL

Frijing, B. W.
De dalende huwelijkslee ftijd in Nederland, door B. W. Frijling. Utrecht: 1969.
(Mededelingen Van Net Sociologisch Inst. van de Rijksuniversiteit te Utrecht, No. 56)
55 pp. Illus. NYPL

PERU

Abarca Fernandez, and R. Ramon
"El vinculo matrimonial en la legislacion y en la sociedad peruana (por) Areouipa," 1966.
185 pp. SUNY

POLAND

Goreck, Jan.
Divorce in Poland; a Contribution to the Society of Law. The Hague: Mouton, 70.
156 pp. NYPL

PORTUGAL

Branco, Deusdado Castelo.
De divorcio por mutuo consentimento na Lei civil vigente. Lisbon, Depositaria: Livraria Petrony, 1969.
24 pp. NYPL

RHODESIA

Goldin, Bennie.
The Problem in Rhodesia: Unhappy Marriage and Divorce. With a foreword by R. H. Christie. Salisbury: Kingstons, 1971.
119 pp. NYPL

RUSSIA

Florkowski, Eicke.
s sowjetische Ehescheidungsrecht. Gottingen: 1967.
517 pp. NYPL

SWEDEN

Helander-Hornlund, Britta.
Skilsmassa. 2. omarb och Rev. uppl.
Stockholm: Forum, 1969.
63 pp. NYPL

Hellsten, Stig.
Om prasts uigselplikt och vigsel av franskilda. Ett herdabrev till praster och forsamlingar. Stockholm: Verbum, 1969.
35 pp.
NYPL

SWITZERLAND

Hinderling, Hans.
Das Schweizerische Ehescheidungsrecht, unter Besonderer. Beruck.
NYPL

Ruttimann, Eugen.
Die Offizialmax:me im Arrgauischen Ehescheidungsprozess. Zurich: Buchdruckerei Akeret, 1968.
108 pp. NYPL

UNION OF SOUTH AFRICA

Hahlo, H. R.
The South African Law of Husband and Wife, with an appendix on Jurisdiction and Conflict

of Laws by Ellison Kahn. Cape Town: Juta, 1969.
745 pp. NYPL

Kloppers, H.P.
Native Divorce Courts' Guide to Practice and Procedure. Cape Town: Juta, 1955.
109 pp.

South Africa Bureau of Statistics. Statistieke van Egskeidings, 1962 en Uroere Jare. Statistics of Divorces, 1962 and earlier years.
Pretoria: Staatsdrucker, 1966.
22 pp. NYPL

WEST PAKISTAN

Chowdhury, Obaidul Hug.
The Muslim Family Laws Ordinana with West Pakistan Family Courts Act (with rules), Dissolution of Muslim Marriages Act & Child Marriage Restraint Act. Dacca: Dacca Law Reports, 1969.
103 pp. NYPL